THE SEVEN DEADLY SINS OF MANAGEMENT

THE SEVEN DEADLY SINS OF MANAGEMENT

HOW TO BE A VIRTUOUS MANAGER

Jonathan Ellis and René Tissen

P
PROFILE BOOKS

First published in 2003 by
Profile Books Ltd
58A Hatton Garden
London ECIN 8LX
www.profilebooks.co.uk

Copyright © Jonathan Ellis and René Tissen 2003

10 9 8 7 6 5 4 3 2 1

Typeset in Bembo by
MacGuru Ltd
info@macguru.org.uk
Printed and bound in Great Britain by
Clays, Bungay, Suffolk

The moral right of the authors has been asserted.

A CIP catalogue record for this book is available from the British Library.

ISBN 1 86197 526 0

To Igor and Maro
Our insightful and inspiring partners

Contents

Foreword

The profession of manager is falling into disrepute. Due to their own actions, managers – and management – are losing their credibility. They are frequently touched by arrogance and pride, convinced that their way is the only option. Practice may prove them wrong – but they will be the last to admit any failing.

Companies, they believe, depend on them. They have convinced themselves that they are corporate saviours and that they alone hold the key to corporate salvation.

Today's new breed of managers no longer manage companies; they manage careers. How often have we read of excessive salary increases? Of new stock options? Little can be more offensive than the board of Enron taking up their stock options while declaring the company bankrupt. And the case of the CEO of an ailing telecom company in Holland giving himself stock options to the value of several million dollars – despite the poor condition of the company – shows that this vice is universal.

Greed is alive and well and living in corporate boardrooms throughout the world.

Today's managers do little to improve their image. They shout that they are right – even when the weight of the evidence proves them wrong. They refuse to listen to advice that runs contrary to their own gut feelings, convinced that they are divinely inspired. They rush into decisions that clearly show how little they understand of their companies' actual business.

Lack of knowledge is no reason for embarrassment.

Certainly, today's high-flyers are faced with enormous challenges. Many companies are plagued with problems that are so new that managers have rarely encountered them before. Yet the tired old solutions that are trotted out do not justify the enormous price tags managers feel justified hanging on themselves. But as long as the share price increases, who cares?

The question on many people's lips is: are managers there for their companies? Or for their egos?

A new mentality?

This book was born largely out of frustration. Not a day seemed to pass without some report of a new acquisition, a new batch of redundancies, yet another (generally new) managing director declaring that shareholder value would be the main goal of his policy.

We wondered whether the business community had fully understood that we had moved out of the Industrial Economy into the Knowledge-based Economy.

To us it seemed as if too many managers were continuing along the same old paths. Paths that had not led to any lasting success in the past, but which many of them appeared intent on following no matter what the signposts were saying. We became convinced that managers were simply refusing to learn from their own mistakes.

And so we defined our Seven Deadly Sins.

We would dearly like to think that these are the only sins that management are guilty of. Yet we know this is not the case. We could list a whole lot more – as, we feel sure, you could. And you are therefore quite entitled to ask why we chose these specific Seven Deadly Sins rather than any of the other sins on the list.

The Seven Deadly Sins discussed here all appear at first to be legitimate management practices. Yet each of them betrays a mentality that is firmly rooted in the past. And this is what makes them suspect.

The Knowledge-based Economy is a totally different ball game. It is being played by new stars, according to new rules. Traditional management concepts have no place here. Yet with only five overs to play, many managers are still trying to force a scrum.

And then they wonder why even the home-crowd starts jeering.

A word about gender

The observant reader (we mean you, of course) will notice that we refer to managers throughout the book as 'he'. We could have followed politically correct practice and written 'he or she'; but we decided against it. Not because we wished to ignore the many women in business, but rather because we are convinced that the sinners are generally male.

A recent study conducted on behalf of the Dutch government

by a research organisation called Opportunity in Business found that of the twenty-five largest Dutch companies surveyed (together employing more than 350,000 people), 75 per cent reported a substantial increase (in excess of 20 per cent) in the 'outflow' of women executives. Women, the study shows, dislike the culture at the top of these companies. Many feel that they have to give up too much of their own identities and too many of their own views. Ultimately, they simply do not think it is worth it. What's more, those (few) women who stay increasingly circulate among these twenty-five companies in search of a better culture. And after a while most of them, too, decide to resign and withdraw from business altogether.

These results perhaps explain why, of the top 100 companies quoted on the FTSE index, only one – yes, one! – has a top female executive.

In the management Garden of Eden, Eve, for once, is less guilty than Adam.

A wonderful opportunity

Today there is a change in attitude towards management, and business practices are being held up to scrutiny. And there is the growing feeling – even in America, that bastion of free enterprise – that running a company should be considered something of an honour. Certainly, such a position gives managers – at least those who make their mark with creative thinking – a wonderful opportunity to become part of a highly successful elite.

There are risks in management. But no more than in any other job. We no longer live in a world in which life-long employment can be guaranteed to anyone. And people tend to forget even the most high-profile manager of the month sooner than he imagines.

Today's managers must understand that old wine will never keep in new bottles. Past solutions will not cut it in the present environment. The ability to change, to concentrate on creating an organisation in which people are central, is the determining factor for success.

Think about it

This book does not contain the latest management theory. It does not discuss a new hype. It doesn't even tell you what you should do. All it does is hold some widely believed ideas against the light. If we do nothing more than make you think, we have achieved our aim.

Acknowledgements

No book is ever written in a vacuum. There are many people who contribute, knowingly or not, to the development of ideas and thoughts. There are, however, several individuals we would like to acknowledge here for their special contribution to our work.

Siemen Jongedijk is everyone's dream of a research assistant. His ability to track down articles and facts – and contribute his own ideas and suggestions – is second to none.

Thanks also to Daniel Andriessen and Frank Lekanne Deprez; their encouragement and support over the years cannot be overestimated.

And finally, special thanks to Hans Ritman – our original publisher who is prepared to take risks; he has become a special friend.

Jonathan Ellis and René Tissen

Introduction

Who's the saint in the management team?

Pride, envy, gluttony, lust, wrath, covetousness and sloth. The Seven Deadly Sins. Few of us go through our lives avoiding them. We all feel a twinge of envy when the neighbour drives up in a new car. We all feel pride at a job well done. We all lust after something or somebody at some time in our lives. We all want more than we already have. We all feel entitled to 'do nothing' at the weekend. We all get furious when we are treated unfairly (unfairly, that is, in our own eyes). And most of us would love to have our superior's job. The Seven Deadly Sins are inescapable. We commit them before we even realise it.

Business today is being hoodwinked. We accept, at face value, concepts that seem genetically determined. Many companies have adopted, albeit silently and often without being fully aware of the fact, a style of management that is 'in their genes', a style of management that is determined by culture, tradition, inertia and upbringing. And because it is almost locked up in the company's DNA, it proves resistant – so managers firmly believe – to hypes, fashions and new concepts. Managers continue doing things in the way they have always done them. It makes them feel comfortable, in charge. But it also makes them unaware of the sins they are committing.

Much of business nowadays is based on the Seven Deadly Sins. Managers are encouraged to be greedy (avarice), to want ever-better results (lust), to get the better of the competition (wrath), to own everything they can (gluttony), to hoard knowledge (covetousness), to do things in the way they have always been done (sloth) and above all to believe totally in their own abilities (pride).

The events following 11 September have shown that there is more to corporate life than money and technology. The ability of competitors to forget competition and offer a helping hand to people whom they now recognised as colleagues shows that business and corporate life can have a soul. But this does not make up for the many aspects of business that have evolved in a way that is detrimental to success. It does not redress the balance – the *im*balance – between the chiefs and the Indians – today, companies employ three times the number of managers that they did ten years ago. There is an increasing hierarchy in companies, an ever-larger number of layers of authority, but there is no increase in authority and responsibility to match the growing increase in control. Companies have praised democratic principles – yet created a world in which people still work like ants.

In this book we look at the Seven Deadly Sins of Management. You may very well be surprised at the sins we discuss here. Surely, we can hear you say, they are all simply part of modern business practice. And that's true – just as the Seven Deadly Sins are part of normal, everyday life. But that doesn't mean that they are any less harmful. For just as the Seven Deadly Sins conspire to destroy our soul, so the Seven Deadly Sins of Management conspire to destroy our business. Commit the sins if you will — but you will do so at your own peril. Worse still, by committing the sins you will put your company at risk. And endanger the future of all the people who depend on your company for their living.

The First Deadly Sin

Lust in the Boardroom

Create shareholder value – no matter what it costs

Y̶ou've worked hard. You've overcome all those nasty obstacles that envious colleagues have laid in your way – and now you've reached the boardroom. The jealousy, envy and malice that you felt towards your colleagues (those enemies trying to beat you to your rightful place) are now replaced with a lust for gain. You've been awarded a big salary. But it is the shares option that you negotiated that is going to be the big winner – as long as you make sure the market value of your company goes sky high. So what do you do? That's right: you create shareholder value. Well, you can always say you're doing it for the good of the company …

Sin-O-Meter for Lust

Do you suffer from the deadly sin of lust? Are you allowing self-interest to colour your business judgement? Answer the following questions honestly (if you dare), and discover your lust rating.

1 What do you check first on Monday mornings: a) last week's sales figures; b) your press release on profit projections; c) your company's share price?
2 You already own stock options in your company. Do you want: a) more; b) a lot more; c) as many as you can get your hands on?
3 A division is showing a loss for the third consecutive quarter. Do you: a) discuss the innovation policy with the divisional COO; b) get in an interim manager to cut costs; c) sell it?
4 Tomorrow you will announce the quarterly results. This evening, do you go out to dinner with: a) your significant other; b) your trader; c) your PR manager?
5 R&D have developed a breakthrough technology; they are now asking for a development budget of $5 million. Do you: a) ROTFLOL*; b) call a board meeting; c) put off the decision to next quarter?
6 Your company's share price is falling. Do you: a) issue a press release promising future profits; b) set a new, earlier deadline for the introduction of a new product; c) take the financial director out to dinner?
7 You are going to address your first shareholders' meeting. Do you announce: a) that shareholder value is your number-one priority; b) that you are planning to concentrate on increasing

---

*Roll on the Floor Laughing Out Loud.

customer satisfaction; c) that you will do everything to improve profits from operations?

8 An acquaintance asks you for investment advice. Do you: a) tell him to invest in a healthy company; b) wink and tell him to watch the newspapers for an important announcement from your company; c) give him the address of schwab.com?

9 You are approached with the offer of a new job. Do you first: a) ask about the company's operating profit; b) negotiate your stock options; c) ask about the company's potential?

10 Your company closes the year with a substantial loss. Do you: a) start a drive to enter new markets; b) blame cheap imports; c) announce a company-wide reorganisation?

Scores

1   a) 0; b) 5; c) 3
2   a) 1; b) 3; c) 8
3   a) 1; b) 4: c) 6
4   a) 2; b) 8; c) 5
5   a) 14; b) 1: c) 4
6   a) 4; b) 1; c) 3
7   a) 6; b) 1; c) 0
8   a) 0; b) 7; c) 2
9   a) 2; b) 20; c) 0
10 a) 1; b) 3; c) 8

0 ━━━━━━━━━━━━━━━━━━━━━━━━━━━━━━ 80

Where are you on the scale? The farther you are to the right, the nearer you are to Purgatory!

'Never before in the history of business have top executives and financial professionals been so committed to the creation of value for their shareholders. And never before have shareholders been so diverse and difficult to please.' *Shareholder Value Magazine*[1] is a publication dedicated to only one thing: offering advice to investors on which companies are offering the best returns. It reflects one of the most important trends in today's business environment: putting the satisfaction of shareholders before almost anything else.

Of course, in the US, it is the legal responsibility of every board of management to optimise the value of their company for the good of the shareholders. In Europe, many companies prefer to talk about 'stakeholder value', including in this their responsibility not only to shareholders, but also to customers, suppliers, employees and society. Yet even here many CEOs are eager to place shareholder value at the very top of their list of priorities.

The question is: why did shareholder value become such a hot item at the end of the twentieth century? And is it still such a major priority in business thinking today?

If you can count your money, then you're not really wealthy.

– Paul Getty

What is my company worth?

As we moved out of the Industrial Economy into the Knowledge-based Economy, so it became increasingly difficult to know what a company was really worth. Traditional accountancy procedures could accurately assess the worth of a company that was heavy with tangible assets. The more factories, machinery, plants and office buildings a company owned, the greater its intrinsic value. It was like the family silver – it was always there to fall back on. Profits from operations may have varied; the value of the family silver generally didn't.

But in the 1980s and 1990s, many companies operating in traditional sectors began to experience increasing difficulties. Diseconomies of scale and the growing inflexibility of dedicated assembly-line processes triggered a period of rationalisation. In order to create 'a lean and mean operation', more and more operations were farmed out to external sources. The tangible assets a company owned no longer reflected that company's ability to compete. The traditional balance sheet had become a poor indicator of a company's value. Companies were no longer judged on what they owned but on what they were able to do. The manager of a semiconductor company remarked, 'We're becoming so successful, we're moving into smaller premises.'

Many companies – particularly those in cutting-edge technologies – began searching for new ways of assessing their intrinsic value. There was a growing understanding that the value of intangible assets – knowledge, patents, business know-how – had a far greater impact on a company's earning potential than the number of offices that company owned.

But the question still remained, where do we go to find out our company's value?

> *Lust is to the other passions what the nervous fluid is to life;*
> *it supports them all, lends strength to them all …*
> *ambition, cruelty, avarice, revenge, are all founded on lust.'*
> – Marquis de Sade

Business barometer?

The answer was the stock market. But that market had changed significantly. A new breed of traders had emerged, who saw the stock market as a place to make big profits. Of course, you could argue that that had always been its role. But there was something more: the stock market was always seen as a business barometer – an indication of the (true) state of a company.

In the Industrial Economy, a company's share price was usually regarded as an indication of its health. A rise in the share price indicated to investors that the company had done well and that it would – all being well – continue to do well in the future. The share price was based on reported earnings, profits on operations, a well-filled portfolio, strong assets and a whole range of other historic data.

In the Knowledge-based Economy, all that has changed: today the share price has become an indication of a company's wealth. In the 1960s and 1970s, about 25 per cent of the differences in share prices could be attributed to differences in reported earnings; by the 1980s and 1990s, this figure had dropped to less than 10 per cent. And it went even further: the share price was not as much an indication of a company's present wealth than of its predicted wealth. Nowadays the higher the share price, the greater the expectations the market has for a particular company. And the more promises a CEO makes, the higher the share price is likely to become. CEOs have learned that lust is one thing that traders in the market fully understand.

All of this has resulted in a widening gap between the declared book value of a company and its market (read: stock market) value. In fact, between 1973 and 1993, the average market-to-book value ratio for US corporations increased from 0.82 to 1.692. And in the period 1981–93, when US companies acquired a company they paid on average 4.4 times the book value of that company.

As a consequence of this trend, owners of newly floated companies suddenly discovered they had become multimillionaires overnight. When Dreamworks SKG was launched, it had declared assets of just $250 million; the market valued it at over $2 billion.[2] Steven Spielberg, Jeffrey Katzenberg and David Geffen must have become very grateful market enthusiasts. After the introduction of Windows 95, Microsoft – an $8 billion company – saw its shares shoot up to $100 billion, making it worth more than either Chrysler or Boeing – and creating many multimillionaire secretaries. Netscape, a $17 million company with just fifty employees, went public and, by the end of the first day, was valued at $3 billion.[3] The same fate awaited owners of the many dot.com companies – the stock market proved eager to buy the emperor's new clothes. But today many of those same owners are realising – with understandable regret – that shares do not retain their value in the way that the family silver did. The market's lust for a quick buck has sent many companies straight into bankruptcy.

> *Lust gratifies its flames in the chambers of the sacristans*
> *more often than in the houses of ill-fame.*
> – Marcus Minucius Felix (2nd or 3rd century AD)

The new market economy

Today's ever-powerful stock market has become more – much, much more – than a simple barometer. It is no longer a passive observer of business; it is an active participant. It has become the Supreme Court of Enterprise. Its decisions are final; companies are made and broken overnight, with cool, calculating indifference.

In such a situation, you ignore shareholders at your peril. Indeed, as *Shareholder Value Magazine* says, 'Nearly every critical business decision today hinges on shareholder value: it drives the day-to-day agenda of every CEO, CFO, investor relations officer and corporate strategist ... managing the expectations of Wall Street analysts, money managers and individual investors is as important as the management of a company's revenue growth and profitability.'[4]

And so market-directed companies are becoming *stock*-market-directed companies; market-responsive strategies become *stock*-market-responsive strategies; market satisfaction is becoming *stock*-market satisfaction; market leader is becoming *stock*-market leader; and the market economy is becoming the *stock*-market economy.

But there is a snake in the grass: while the stock market may make your company wealthy, it can never generate cash flow for you. And you, as a manager, become caught up in a balancing act: generating wealth on paper – and generating cash in the bank. Balancing the wealth created by projections of future earnings and the cash generated by present products and services. For while the stock market is more interested in future promise, your customers expect delivery today.

> *The lust for comfort, that stealthy thing that enters the house a guest,*
> *and then becomes a host, and then a master.*
>   – Kahlil Gibran

Everybody's doing it

Nevertheless, more and more CEOs are coming out on the side of shareholder value. Some may say this is self-interest: as many salaries include generous stock options, it is only in the CEOs' own interests to ensure that the share price is always moving upwards. The wealthier their company is perceived to be, the wealthier the CEO becomes. Lust is the order of the day in boardrooms throughout the world.

A glance at the annual reports of some large companies is enough to confirm this. Íslandbanki: 'The mission of the Bank is to increase shareholder value by offering households and corporations outstanding financial services and providing customers with value-adding solutions.'[5] Cadbury Schweppes: 'Shareholder return is committed to double every four years.'[6] 'Arch Coal is dedicated to being a market-driven global leader in the coal industry and to creating superior long-term shareholder value.'[7] 'Hillenbrand Industries' primary mission is to manage our portfolio of businesses and leadership talent to increase shareholder value.'[8] PA Consulting: 'The stated mission of our senior management is to manage for and increase shareholder value.'[9]

And we're willing to bet that *your* company says something very similar.

You can't ignore it

The lure of shareholder value is hard to ignore. Yet it is surprising that the tools that many CEOs use for achieving this value were forged not in the present Knowledge-based Economy, but rather in the furnaces of the Industrial Economy. In many cases, they are blunt and brutal instruments – but none the less effective.

One such instrument is divestment. Divisions that are no longer making a healthy contribution to the 'core business' or do not provide a 'strategic fit' or are not 'competitive' are sold off, the income providing a healthy boost to the balance sheet. Operations are scaled down, as manufacturing capacity is divested, freeing a company to use 'strategic suppliers' (often the units that were once part of the company) without having to carry the overheads demanded by such operations or allowing them to relocate manufacturing in low-cost countries. Research effort is focused on incremental rather than breakthrough improvement, thus reducing the investments required for long-term projects. And, of course, there is the ultimate weapon of redundancies as a result of a further 'rationalisation' of products and operations.

Financial engineering

We believe that much of this can be termed 'financial engineering'. It is the work of bookkeepers, rather than managers. It is lusting after the quick buck. It is painting an ever-brighter financial picture. Yet it is viewed as laudable by the stock market. Not, of course, that anybody would accuse traders of the sin of lust.

When Cor Boonstra left his job with Sara Lee to become President of Royal Philips Electronics, he stated that his policy would be focused on creating shareholder value. And many of the policies he implemented, in this highly diversified Fortune Top 100 company that employs over 200,000 people around the world, were exactly those measures we have mentioned above. In the 1998 annual report he writes (the emphasis is ours):

- We have continued the process of refocusing the company.
- We have continued to streamline our manufacturing operations.
- *We have used part of our surplus funds to boost shareholder value while we look for the most profitable use for them in the long term.*
- We have continued our drive to reduce costs.[10]

The following year, Boonstra was pleased to announce:

- We used our net cash position to return some 71.5 billion to shareholders while reducing the number of outstanding shares by 8 per cent.
- *The share price rose by 136 per cent during the year, adding €24 billion to our market value.*[11]

Where did the money come from?

A closer analysis of the Philips policy shows that the greatest source of income during those years came from the sale of Polygram – the Philips entertainment division – to Seagram and the sales of some forty other divisions, including the IT division Origin, the passive components division – that operated independently as BCcomponents – and participation in activities as diverse as mobile phones and car radios. Boonstra summed this up in the 1998 report:

We have made real progress in realigning our operations, and this has had a dramatic impact on our balance sheet, resulting in a net cash surplus. Although cash flow excluding the net proceeds of the sale and purchase of business interests and non-current financial assets was considerably down on last year's record figure, it still showed a level of 1.6 billion Dutch guilders.[12]

In other words, the improvements didn't come from better operations, more sales, greater consumer confidence or better customer satisfaction. In fact, there was a downturn in all these areas. No, the money came from financial engineering. A perfect example of selling off the family silver. But Boonstra did all this to increase shareholder value. As he states in the 1999 annual report: 'Most of all, on behalf of the board, I would like to thank you, as one of our shareholders, for your continued support. We are very much aware that it is the personal trust shown in the company by you and your fellow shareholders that makes the whole exciting Philips enterprise possible.'[13]

Slave to Wall Street

In today's litany of corporate failures, the companies concerned – Enron, Global Crossing, Xerox, Lucent, Qwest – all have one thing in common: they became the slaves of Wall Street. They became slaves to promising growth – and found creative ways to deliver that growth. Enron included future earnings on a twenty-year contract in one budget year, declaring income that would not be seen for many years. But it certainly kept Wall Street happy.

Growth targets had to be met, no matter how. As Wall Street darling Lucent promised growth that many people inside the company thought unrealistic, creative bookkeeping pulled forward sales from future quarters 'by offering steep discounts and wildly generous financing arrangements. "As we got further and further behind," Chairman Henry Schacht [the newly appointed CEO] later explained, "we did more and more discounting." '[14]

Ultimately, the Lucent bubble burst and lost more than 80 per cent of its value. Schacht commented, 'Stock price is a by-product; stock price isn't a driver. And anytime I've seen any of us lose sight of that, it has always been a painful experience.'[15]

Ambition is the ecclesiastical lust.

– Daniel Noonan

Who pulls the strings?

Can stock markets be the final judge and jury in business matters? Do shareholders make business possible? Certainly, they are a very important player in the total corporate framework. But they are *enablers* of business. They provide the cash, and they rightly expect to see returns on their investments – so, in this sense, they do, indeed, make business possible. But so do banks. So do suppliers. So do employees. So do customers. Concentrating on shareholders means paying less attention to all these other enablers of business.

Shareholders see the stock market as their business arena – the place where they face competition, design strategies, make profits, wheel and deal.

Much of the strategy they adopt is based on expectations. If they *expect* a company to perform well, they will invest in shares in that company. If they *expect* a company to underperform, they will sell any shares they have in that company. But these expectations are ultimately fulfilled not by shareholders, but by other stakeholders in a company.

Shareholders may have high expectations for your company – but that means *you* have do your part. *You* have to go out and sell your products or services. *You* have to put in place healthy business processes. *You* have to attract customers. *You* have to find the employees with the knowledge to help you make it happen. If you don't, then shareholder expectations will plummet. And so will the value of your company. Although whether that is as important to a CEO as the value of his share options is a matter we leave to the reader to decide.

'Hardly original'

This is what the *Financial Times* had to say about the strategy adopted by L'Oréal's chief executive: 'The strategy Mr Owen-Jones pursues – focus on a constellation of star brands and then push them into faster growing developing markets – is hardly original in the fast-moving consumer goods industry but it has proved extremely effective.'[16]

L'Oréal, a big name in the cosmetics industry, has become one of the darlings of the stock market. Yet this has little to do with expectations; rather it is the constant and consistent performance of the company that has gained it its premium rating. In the words again of the *Financial Times*:

> It is the consistency of L'Oréal's financial performance that is its most remarkable feature: it has achieved double-digit profit growth

*every year for the past sixteen years. Net profits in 2000, of €1
billion ($900 million) on sales of €12.7 billion, were double those of
1995, which in turn were twice those of 1990. The market has
rewarded this consistent growth record with a premium rating that
leaves no scope for disappointment. L'Oréal shares trade on about
46 times forecast 2001 earnings, more than twice the price/earning
ratio of the market as a whole. Living up to expectations is
L'Oréal's greatest challenge.*[17]

Here, again, we see 'expectations'. But these are based on the
healthy performance the company has shown over sixteen years.
Past success is projected into future expectations. L'Oréal has produced high shareholder value by making exceptional profits year
in, year out.

> *Their insatiable lust for power is only equalled by
> their incurable impotence in exercising it.*
>
> – Winston Churchill

'Shareholders aren't everything'

In February 1997, *Fortune* published an article entitled 'Shareholders aren't everything'. In his interview with John Kay, Director
Designate of Oxford University's School of Management Studies,
Erin Davis states: 'The horizon of managers is getting shorter by
the minute. CEOs seem only to be interested in the shareholder
value of today's shareholders. This will not last. Investments in
people and knowledge need to be made. This will not please the
shareholders.' And Kay himself argues that a company's purpose is

'producing goods and services people want. Business is about providing employment, providing value for customers, for developing skills of employees, for developing capabilities of suppliers – as well as earning money for shareholders'.[18] A successful business creates value, he maintains. And he believes that a necessary condition for creating value is a win–win sharing between shareholders, employees, customers and other stakeholders.

Certainly, Kay is not the only commentator who has warned against ignoring the interests of stakeholders in a lustful desire to create shareholder value. Many see the detrimental effects an over-concentration on shareholders can have. Motivation, for example, can be seriously harmed if employees are constantly being told that they are doing everything for the shareholders. Do the shareholders buy our products? they wonder. Do we no longer do things for our customers? they ask. Are we market-driven or stock-market-driven?

Wealthy or healthy?

What many commentators are saying is that you have to create shareholder value *by making your company healthy*. It's all very well to have a wealthy company – wealthy, that is, based on share prices – but it is an entirely different matter to be healthy.

When the dot.com bubble burst, investors suffered enormous losses. Share prices plummeted. Billions of dollars were wiped out, seemingly overnight. Some of the world's wealthiest companies were suddenly destitute. And shareholders had, once more, to accept the old cliché, 'There's no such thing as a sure bet'.

In retrospect, most people understand that many dot.com companies were vastly overvalued. Sure, there were great expectations.

But there was no pay-off. The CEO of Sun Computers, Scott McNealy, commented wryly to a group of New York investors about dot.com companies: 'The value of the cars in the parking lot exceeds the company's revenues by a factor of four.' Where did they get the money to buy all those cars? Simply by promising more than they ever delivered.

Ultimately, revenue from operations is the thing that counts. Higher profits, solid investments, customer-oriented development: these are the true indicators of a company's health. Financial re-engineering may help create the illusion of a wealthy company – it can never ensure that wealth equals health.

Managers today must once again return to what they do best: leverage their companies' competencies to produce products and services that appeal to the customer and create value. If they do that, then shareholder value will follow automatically.

The cart before the horse

There's nothing wrong with creating shareholder value. In fact, there's everything *right* about striving to ensure a healthy return for the people who provide some of the capital to make your operations possible. It only becomes a deadly sin when it takes priority over everything else. Focusing on shareholder value to the exclusion of operations, investments, motivating the workforce, creating strategic alliances with partners and suppliers is, indeed, a deadly sin. It is putting the cart before the horse.

Today, as companies are facing the enormous challenges of operating in a world where intangible assets are ever-more important, they must stop their single-minded focus on shareholder value. Instead, they must recognise that stakeholder value – in which shareholders are one of the parties – must take priority. Knowledge resides in the heads of employees – and thus employees must be valued much more than at any other time in the past. Managers must focus on creating strategic alliances, participating in networks of knowledge, if they are to satisfy customers that demand more than ever before.

Earlier in this chapter we discussed the operations of Philips and L'Oréal. The former concentrated on shareholder value, but did not generate higher profits – its share price has since shown a steady decline. On the other hand, L'Oréal concentrated on generating profits from operations, and they have been rewarded by a steadily rising share price. One went for wealth – the other for health.

Some love is fire, some love is rust – but the purest, cleanest love is lust.

– St Augustine

Lust in the boardroom

Nobody gets to the boardroom without lust. Many managers lust for success. Lust to rise above the average. Lust to be better than the rest. Lust, if directed properly, can be a great virtue.

But when lust for self-enrichment is allowed to run rampant, then it's another matter.

In today's world, the drive to create shareholder value all too often goes hand in hand with a lust to increase the value of a CEO's own share holdings. It is a self-interested lust – and that makes it a sin.

A sin that can be deadly to the company.

CASES

The sinner: Railtrack

Lust in the boardroom? You bet. Railtrack, now in receivership, owes its demise to a single fact: placing shareholder value above everything else. While shareholders enjoyed dividend after dividend and a rise in the price of their shares from an initial £3.80 to a high of £17.68, passengers on the railways were expected to take the 16.37 to Hell!

When the railways were privatised, in the 1993 Railways Act, it was decided that the operation of the infrastructure should be placed in the hands of a public company. Railtrack was set up as a public company in 1996; it owned the national railway infrastructure and levied fees from the railway companies for its use. It was responsible not only for the maintenance of the tracks, but also for all investments in the infrastructure, whether those investments were funded by Railtrack itself or by third parties. Its status as one of the UK's largest 100 companies, the explanation went, would better allow it to attract vital investment money from the City.

From the start, Railtrack operated at a profit. But rather than using this money for upgrading the decrepit tracks and expanding the infrastructure – something essential as the number of passengers using the railways grew and the operators were constantly faced with lines that were overcrowded, making it almost impossible to maintain a regular timetable – the company used it to pay out dividends to the shareholders.

And then, in 1999, one of the worst train disasters in UK history happened at Hatfield. The cause: the poor state of the tracks. The costs of upgrading the tracks after Hatfield have proved enormous.

23

And then there are the costs of the West Coast line – now running nearly £5 billion above the original estimates. In 2001, Railtrack reported losses for the first time. The share price tumbled. The company turned, cap in hand, to the government. But they had signed their own death warrant. At the end of 2001, Railtrack went into administration. Shareholders, who had enjoyed all those dividends at the expense of passenger service and, ultimately, passengers' lives, were left with worthless scraps of paper.

Now the operations of Railtrack are being taken over by a new company, Network Rail. But it is a not-for-profit organisation; all profits will be put back into the rail network. And the shareholders? Well, they were finally offered £2.50 per share. This was, the government said, intended to insure that Network Rail could get on with its job as quickly as possible without being bogged down in a long-running court battle. But for the long-suffering travelling public, the price of lust will be paid for many years to come.

The saint: Cadbury Schweppes

People investing in Cadbury Schweppes have found out that there are some sweet things in life, because the company has turned into a major moneymaker for shareholders. Not by icing the figures, but by solid business strategy and effort.

In 1997, Cadbury Schweppes made a public commitment to what it called 'shareowner value'. The company set itself targets of increasing earnings per share by 10 per cent per annum, to generate at least £150 million of free cash flow, and strive to double total shareowner returns every four years. The results for 1997–2000 show that the company came very close to achieving these challenging targets: underlying earnings per share grew by 11 per cent, free cash flow averaged £252 million and total shareowner return grew by 84 per cent.

What makes Cadbury Schweppes different from other companies that publicly promise shareholder value is that here such a promise is not an aim in itself, but rather the result of a very clearly defined market-driven strategy. In 1999, the company generated beverage sales worth £1 billion in 160 markets where its presence was modest; this enabled it to focus its resources in three key markets: Europe, the United States and Australia. In these three areas, it has focused on its core growth markets of confectioneries and beverages, aiming to achieve a robust and sustainable market position built on strong brands. This has been supported by franchising operations and product-directed innovations, and by enhancing their market position through acquisitions or disposals based on strategy, value creation and availability.

In addition, Cadbury Schweppes has developed an important financial tool that it calls the 'Managing for Value' programme. Using this programme, the company measures value creation in terms of economic profit. Here the cost of capital – both that provided by shareholders and that obtained by the company itself – is taken into account when calculating the economic profitability of the business. This, the company, believes is preferable to more traditional calculating methods such as operating profit after tax or earnings per share – since it takes into account the full cost of the capital used to generate profits.

Thanks to this clear focus on managing market-driven growth and profitability, Cadbury Schweppes has generated exceptional shareholder value. In its next four-year plan, the company is maintaining its commitment to shareowner value. At the same time, however, it is placing great emphasis on growth and management is being encouraged to focus on promoting 'good', that is, profitable, growth through innovation – in products and packaging – and extending the availability of its products.

So if you want a tip about where to invest your money – think 'Sch – you know who'.

The Second Deadly Sin

Wrath on the High Street

Attack the competition – with anything it takes

B usiness is like soccer: a game for gentlemen played by hooligans. And anyone who thinks that playing fair will bring its true rewards deserves to be in the Vatican, not the boardroom. No, if you're going to succeed you have to play to beat the competition. Of course, it's all very well to innovate your own products, but the quickest way is to copy the others. Beat them at their own game. Knock them for six. And if you have to resort to undercover methods – who's going to care?

Sin-O-Meter for Wrath

Do you enjoy flexing your competitive muscles? Are you engaged in a take-no-prisoners war with other players in your market segment? Answer these questions honestly and discover how much wrath you put into your daily business dealings.

1   A major competitor introduces a new product. Do you: a) call your development department and ask them when the hell your version of the product will be ready; b) send your secretary out to buy one; c) get marketing to check their customer-preference data?

2   You are developing a new product. Do you pay most attention to: a) market research; b) competitive analysis; c) reports from that detective agency you hired two weeks ago?

3   Your competitor announces that he will be introducing a new operating system. Do you: a) make an appointment to discuss a licensing agreement; b) tell R&D to come up with something different (but not necessarily better); c) buy shares in your competitor's company?

4   You hear that your leading competitor is launching a new product. Do you: a) offer your competitor's research director a job; b) plan a major advertising campaign to coincide with the launch; c) cut the prices of your own products by 10 per cent?

5   The market in which you operate has only two major players. Is your most important weapon: a) espionage; b) innovation; c) sabotage?

6   Your leading competitor introduces a 'me-too' product. Do you: a) run an ad saying 'Imitation is the highest form of flattery'; b) fire your security manager; c) bring forward the release date of your next generation product?

7 You are addressing your annual sales conference. Do you tell your sales people: a) that they have to sell, sell, sell; b) that they should provide more feedback on customer requirements; c) that they should go out there and destroy, destroy, destroy?

8 Industry figures show that your company has slipped to the number two spot. Do you: a) commission a detailed analysis of number one's weaknesses; b) fire the commercial director; c) reassess your product portfolio in the light of a recent consumer survey?

9 Your major distributor complains that your products are no longer offering competitive benefits. Do you: a) change distributors; b) ask him for suggestions for improving your products; c) instruct marketing to implement a company-wide customer-feedback strategy?

10 Your major competitor introduces a service that you are convinced will be a non-starter. Do you: a) laugh all the way to the bank; b) introduce a 'me-too' service; c) give your staff detailed information about why your company will not be introducing a similar service?

Scores

1 a) 3; b) 5; c) 1
2 a) 2; b) 6; c) 8
3 a) 2; b) 8; c) 8
4 a) 6; b) 3; c) 4
5 a) 10; b) 1; c) 12
6 a) 3; b) 7; c) 2
7 a) 3; b) 1; c) 9
8 a) 5; b) 9; c) 2
9 a) 4; b) 2; c) 2
10 a) 4; b) 6; c) 1

0 ══════════════════════════════════════ 80

Where are you on the scale? The farther you are to the right, the nearer you are to Purgatory!

'They can't predict the future, but corporate spies can help managers understand what competitors have up their sleeves, information that they can use to deploy scarce resources, price products and services, modify strategies and avoid costly mistakes. "When you're going into a war situation, you don't want to be cutting the budget of the CIA,' says Michael Mace, chief competitive officer at handheld-computer maker Palm Inc."[1]

Business is war. It is all about companies battling with other companies. It is a foray into alien territory. And the spoils of war are enormous profits.

And the best way to win those spoils is to attack the competition. After all, they are after the same spoils. Disable the competition and you are in a better position to enjoy the eventual victory. Take no prisoners. Destroy them.

Within business, competitive analysis and competitive intelligence have always played a vital role. This is understandable – and good business practice. Certainly, in mature markets, with limited opportunities for anything more than incremental improvement, the only way to increase market share – and profits – is to eat into the slice of the pie enjoyed by the competition. Forewarned is forearmed.

As markets mature, so the room for manoeuvre decreases. The cards are already shuffled and dealt. The consumers are already locked into the product. The game is no longer about creating a market, but competing for the favours of a relatively static group of consumers. As maturity increases, so companies are forced to compete for replacements. Improving market share is the only chance of growth. And that can only be achieved by attacking the territory already held by the competition.

Anger is a momentary madness, so control your passion or it will control you.

— Horace

I was angry with my friend:
I told my wrath, my wrath did end.
I was angry with my foe:
I told it not, my wrath did grow.

— William Blake

Attack and be damned

There are many ways of attacking the competition. For example, recently one company did everything possible to discover the launch date of its major competitor's new product and then engineered a major advertising push on the same day, thus greatly reducing the impact the competitor had on the market. This seems an acceptable – and effective – way to defend a market share and prevent a competitor making inroads into the market. On the other hand, one could equally argue that a pre-emptive strike with a new product that offered more than was offered by the competitor would have been an even better approach. Unfortunately, many companies do not have the agility and speed to leverage internal forces to create a new product as quickly as they can create a new advertising campaign!

Much effort is expanded on ensuring that features introduced by a competitor are integrated as quickly as possible into your own products. Although there are perfectly sensible business reasons for this – if your competitor believes customers want an integrated coffee-machine cum alarm clock, then you shouldn't miss the boat – it does condemn a company to play 'catch up' all the time. It is also a quick fix: it allows management to match a product feature for feature, but it has little lasting impact on the market-creating capabilities within a company. But then, all too many companies seem to adopt the attitude that it is better to offer a good imitation than a bad original. After all, the competition does it too.

At its most extreme, this mentality can lead to producing a 'me-too' product and marketing it at a lower price. The aim is to price the competitor out of the market – a much-loved approach by companies with clout and deep pockets. The question that arises is whether this is actually of benefit to anyone. Ultimately, continuous price erosion can only lead to a situation in which a large number of companies decide to cut their losses and retire from the arena altogether. Unfortunately, those few companies that remain will find it very difficult – if not impossible – to make any significant profits at the price levels that the market now has grown to expect. It is virtually impossible to change the direction of a downward spiralling price trend. Customers simply won't accept it. The result? Downsizing, redundancies and restructuring.

If handled carefully and with full understanding of the consequences, such an approach can, however, result in a strategic victory. It certainly did for the Japanese electronics industry in the early 1970s. In retrospect, of course, we know that the price-cutting strategy was backed up by a lean production process that offered companies the ability to produce high-quality, competitive products at low prices. But because established Western companies were unable to match the low-cost production methods with their over-inflated production processes, they cried foul. They were simply unable to match the production standards being set in other parts of the world.

This was also the approach adopted by Toyota when they introduced the Lexus. *Business Week* reported:

> *Toyota Motor Corp.'s (TM) trusty sedans have always been known as reliable, low-maintenance cars – so much so that they command a high resale price when the time has come to upgrade them. A decade ago, Toyota owners may have moved up to a Cadillac or even an entry-level Jaguar or Mercedes-Benz. Not any more. These days, it's just as likely that the next car will be another Toyota, sold under the Lexus badge. In just twelve years since the brand was launched, Lexus has vaulted to the top of a very competitive field. The current record for most trouble-free car in J.D. Power & Associates' survey of new-car quality is held by the Lexus line's flagship LS 430 sedan. The quality edge attracts new buyers, as do Toyota's smart marketing and service at dealerships. How did Toyota go about setting a global benchmark for quality with its Lexus line? 'In building the Lexus, our operating principle has been to cut the margin for error in half and we also went to extremes to rethink the way we made cars,' says Kousuke Shiramizu, global chief of Toyota's luxury-car production.*[2]

All this shows that attacking the competition through price can be successful only if the company initiating the offensive has taken the time and effort to understand its core competencies and has the ability to satisfy to the full the expectations its actions generate in the market.

Men often make up in wrath what they want in reason.
— William Rounseville Alger

Assumption replaces knowledge

One of the most pernicious results of attacking the competition is that it encourages managers to replace knowledge with assumption. If a competitor does something, then it is assumed, there must be a good reason for it. This attitude results all too frequently in 'me-too' actions that are at best precipitous and at worst disastrous — as for example the rush to get on to the web: many managers have embarked on an exercise in e-commerce without taking the necessary time to formulate targets and expected gains from such an action. The assumption that it will be beneficial has replaced the knowledge required for any successful business strategy.

Another example of using assumption rather than knowledge has been the rush to introduce mobile telephones that offer access to the internet. Initial research showed that there was a marginal interest in this new means of communication, and it was 'assumed' — this time by a whole industry — that this interest would increase dramatically when the service was made available. In a mad-hatter rush to attack the competition, many companies have poured money into developing a service that, until now, has proved of little interest to the consumer. Indeed, the latest research figures show that the initial interest has actually declined. You can lead a horse to water …

I spy with my little eye …

Comparative market surveys have always been a common instrument in business. And it is, of course, vital to understand why consumers choose one brand above another. This is different, though, to the situation now emerging, in which companies jump on to every trend, not because they have a deep conviction of their own ability to achieve results in a given area but because there is an assumption that the new trend will lead them to the promised pot of gold.

There are simply not enough pots of gold to go around. But traditional market research is now being replaced by so-called competitive intelligence.

In other words, companies are going into the spy business.

To quote *Business Week* again:

In a recession, competitive intelligence can pay off big. The ranks of legitimate spies have risen dramatically, by over 220 per cent in the past decade, so that more than 5,000 corporate spies are now actively engaged in intelligence activities. Nine out of ten large companies have employees dedicated solely to the competitive-intelligence function, according to Leonard M. Fuld, president and founder of Fuld & Co., a Cambridge (Mass.) intelligence consultant. Most reside in marketing, strategy and information services departments, answering to anyone from mid-level managers to the CEO. Increasingly, corporate intelligence-gatherers are better educated – many have MBAs or professional certification, or have studied corporate spying at the growing number of universities that offer courses in it, including Brigham Young University and the University of Pittsburgh. And the tools at their disposal, including

*search engines, are more sophisticated. Many large US companies
spend upwards of $1 million a year tracking their competitors, and
they build the information right into their sales strategies.[3]*

Certainly the gathering of competitive information can place a
company in a strong position to avert corporate disaster. This was
certainly the case for Texas Instruments. The article continues:

*When executives at Texas Instruments Inc. began suspecting that a
rival might move to acquire Telogy Networks Inc. two years ago, it
set off alarms deep within the company. At the time, Telogy
provided the software for TI's internet telephony hardware, so a
rival's acquisition of the company would have been disastrous. A
half-dozen executives, acting as TI's corporate spies, sprang into
action, quickly contacting Telogy execs and dispatching finance
people to research the company. The 'competitive intelligence' they
developed convinced management that it needed to acquire Telogy
quickly – and safeguard what is now a $100 million business with
enormous growth potential at a time when bright spots on the tech
horizon are few. 'It's a fact: if you snooze, you lose,' says Jeffrey
S. McCreary, senior vice-president for worldwide sales and
marketing. 'Competitive intelligence is your best alarm clock.'[4]*

> *When a man is wrong and won't admit it, he always gets angry.*
> – Haliburton

The spy that got caught in the cold

But some companies take competitive intelligence a little too far.

While such a practice can be defended when one is gathering knowledge about the future, it enters a much greyer area when it means gathering information to damage a competitor. Oracle Corp. did just that when detectives they had hired persuaded janitors to sift through Microsoft's rubbish in search of information that could be used to harm Microsoft in court.

But a much more condemnable action was undertaken by giant Procter & Gamble. They hired spies to keep an eye on the hair-care business of their main competitor Unilever. These spies used all the methods usually seen in action movies rather than in corporate competition. Now the company is trying to settle the resulting dispute with Unilever.

> *Procter & Gamble will again try to reach a settlement with Unilever over their corporate espionage dispute on Tuesday – but any deal between the two consumer goods companies could lead to accusations of anticompetitive behaviour. P&G confessed to Unilever in April that its own rules were breached during an operation to spy on the Anglo-Dutch company's hair-care business. P&G, which makes Pantene Pro-V shampoo, returned more than eighty documents to Unilever following the operation. Its methods included rummaging through litter bins. Last week, Unilever was understood to be demanding that P&G chief executive A.G. Lafley delays certain product launches and submits P&G's hair-care plans for the next two to three years to an independent audit to make sure they do not use confidential information. If no agreement is reached, it is likely that Unilever will sue. Among the information gleaned from the spying operation, P&G is thought to have discovered details of a product planned by Unilever, including the price and advertising budget.[5]*

What makes this case even more surprising is that Procter & Gamble have a long tradition of solid R&D. They can boast about their own laboratories, and they have been instrumental in introducing a whole range of high-quality and extremely successful products. That they feel the need to spy on a competitor seems to fly in the face of this tradition. But it must also be noted that P&G have been having a dry spell in the last few years. As *The Economist* reports: 'Several big established "ideas factories", including 3M, Procter & Gamble and Rubbermaid, have had dry spells recently. Gillette spent ten years and $1 billion developing its new Mach 3 razor; it took a British supermarket only a year or so to produce a reasonable imitation.'[6]

Perhaps even these big names wonder whether such enormous investments in new products – which can be easily copied by less knowledge-intensive companies – is justified. And so they, too, look for the easy option. Better a good copy than a bad original …

Strengths or weaknesses?

So the question arises as to what is the correct and most sustainable strategy: do you continue to attack your competitor's weaknesses, or do you develop a battle-plan based on your own strengths?

In today's competitive markets, the need to understand your own competencies – the abilities that distinguish you from the competition – is becoming increasingly vital. Yet this is the one thing that causes enormous difficulties to even the most successful companies.

An article in *Management Team* reflects:

It is strange how much effort it costs leading companies to define their own strengths. They seem to prefer to expand in areas that have little to do with their core activities. It would seem far more logical to seek expansion in the core business and to use this to reduce costs. This is called believing in yourself and it separates the mediocre from the truly successful.[7]

This belief in yourself is something that is all too lacking in many companies.

And in many managers.

In the pressure-cooker world of the boardroom, all too much emphasis is placed on short-term results. It is more desirable, it would seem, to go for short-term gains rather than long-term sustainability. Managers forget the words of Sun Tzu in *The Art of War*: 'If you sit on the bank long enough, you will see the bodies of your enemies float by.' Who, in today's boardroom, is prepared to tell people – not least ever-demanding shareholders – that they must sit and wait? That management has decided to ignore short-term gains in favour of long-term prosperity?

It is much more invigorating to fight a battle than to build a fortress.

Time out

In ancient China, wars were only ever fought in the summer. Spring was the time for planting – so it would be endangering your future to engage in battle then instead of making provisions for the future. Similarly, war was never waged in autumn, since this would mean allocating human resources who should be used to bring in the harvest to battles.

Today, the corporate war continues unabated. There are no seasons in corporate life. All forces are mobilised at all times; there is no time for sowing or reaping. In other words, we no longer allow ourselves the time to invest in our sustainable future.

A true evaluation of core competencies takes more than a thirty-minute meeting. Nor can it be done by a small team, no matter how gifted the team members are. An evaluation of all aspects of a company's abilities, strengths and weaknesses is a time-consuming affair. It must be undertaken and supported by all layers within the company, for only then can the fundamental strengths be uncovered. Few companies actually embark on this process. However, unless they are prepared to do so, companies will simply be allowing themselves to become rudderless vessels, carried here and there by the unpredictable tides of events.

> *Anger is seldom without argument but seldom with a good one.*
>
> – Lord Halifax

Intel outside?

Intel is a company that has grown used to having things pretty much its own way. It is, as *Business Week* observes, 'a company accustomed to being the only choice in a market.'[8] This has not, however, made the company more aware of its core competencies, nor has it taught it that it can be suicide – even for Intel – to enter markets utterly alien to their core business. *Business Week* continues:

> *For the past three years, Intel has seesawed between product*

shortages and product delays in its core computer-chip business. Piled on top of that have been embarrassing bugs, recalls and overpriced processors that opened the door for rivals. Now, Intel is bracing itself for its worst financial results since it fled the memory-chip business in 1985. Sure, the entire semiconductor industry is in its worst slump in a decade, suffering from overcapacity and weak demand that will cause global chip sales to tumble 34 per cent this year, according to researcher IC Insights. But Intel will take a bigger hit, because it has failed so far to wean itself from dependence on a slowing PC business.

What went wrong?

Critics say [CEO Craig] Barrett has been trying to move Intel into too many new markets, fracturing the company's focus on its core business. Three years ago, he vowed to branch out into communications, info appliances and internet services. His original vision not only called for making chips for networking gear, cell phones and handheld computers, but also for churning out Intel hardware – network servers, Web-surfing devices and routers to guide data over networks. At the same time, Barrett tried to build a services business, with Intel running e-commerce operations for others or dishing up business software to corporate customers over the net. The full scope of his vision has been far from realised. Barrett's invasion into new markets has been even more dismal. So far, some $4 billion of Intel's more than $10 billion in new investments have produced little. This year, Intel stopped making network servers and routers after some of its biggest chip customers, including Dell Computer Corp. (DELL) and Cisco Systems Inc. (CSCO), slapped Barrett's hands for competing against them. In February, Barrett shut down a service for broadcasting shareholder meetings and training sessions over the Web. He shuttered iCat, an

*e-commerce and hosting service for small and midsize businesses.
And he has retreated so far in the information-appliance business
that Intel now markets its Web-surfing devices only in Spain.
'Certainly, Craig's vision looked a lot more attractive a year and a
half, two years ago,' sighs board member David B. Yoffie, a
professor at Harvard Business School.[9]*

Let's face it, if Intel can't define its own competencies, who can?

If you can't define your own strengths, then there is always the alternative: discover the competition's weaknesses. It is a pragmatic approach that might win a battle, but will never win the war.

Still following the leader?

Concentrating on competitors and competition often forces companies to forget the market. They are so anxiously chasing the newest technology, the newest feature, the latest trend, that they forget to look inside and see whether their existing strengths – their core competencies – may not place them in a good position to launch something that does not follow the competition but actually leads the way.

In the airline industry in the mid 1970s, the growth of special tariffs, booking regulations, length–of–stay restrictions and promotions resulted in the same seat being offered for sale at a wide range of prices. Often a person unable to take advantage of the special offers – generally business travellers who could not plan their trips to include a weekend stop-over, or who could not afford not to be able to change flights as circumstances required – would sit next to someone who had paid only a quarter of the price he or she had paid. KLM Royal Dutch Airlines was the first to recognise the potential of business travel and introduced what was called the Triple F – Full Fare Facilities – programme. This laid the foundations for Business Class. Of course, it was not long before other airlines were offering 'me-too' Business Classes and KLM's lead was short-lived. But KLM's Triple F was so innovative that it created a new market segment. And one in which KLM is still a recognised leader.

Anybody can become angry – that is easy; but to be angry with the right person, and to the right degree, and at the right time, and for the right purpose, and in the right way – that is not within everybody's power and is not easy.

– Aristotle

Thrown to the wolves

Competition, they say, helps a company become more agile, more customer-oriented. And indeed it is one of the elements that can be of particular importance in redefining corporate strategy. Yet, all too often, companies are expected to face competition that they have never had to confront before in their lives.

This is the situation many public-owned companies – often monopolies – have had to deal with when the decision has been made to privatise them. Competition on the open market, the reasoning goes, will make them healthier, leaner, meaner and more profitable. And it will make them more customer-friendly.

But in fact these companies frequently fail dismally. What we are witnessing today is that many telecom companies – often emerging from state-owned monopolies – are unable to compete with new-comers, who have less experience in the industry, yet seem to have a better idea of what is going on in the market.

Many monopolies have grown strong by giving the customer what they have to offer, with little concern for what that customer actually needs. They have grown fat by supplying a service that is one of a kind. They have grown strong thanks to a 'take-it-or-leave-it' position in the market place. When faced with competition, such companies simply don't know what to do – and they flounder, wondering what on earth the customer is thinking about.

This is the situation in which the newly privatised postal service in the United Kingdom finds itself. The monopoly it enjoyed for many decades simply did not prepare it for the competition it is facing today. Customers who have at last a choice in their mail-delivery service will no longer accept paying – in advance, of course – for next-day delivery and then finding that their mail is taking a week or more to reach its destination.

Recently, the management announced that the company was going steeply into the red. Estimated losses had reached £1 million a day. Competition had hit the company badly – competition not only from alternative mail deliverers, but also from email and SMS messaging services.

The response? A staff cut of around 20,000 employees.

Will this, however, place the company in a better position to offer high-class customer service? We doubt it. It may cut costs – but we are convinced it will do nothing at all to improve the competitive position of the company. You cannot possibly hope to make a company more competitive by cutting the workforce so drastically.

Yet we also sympathise with management: they have never

before felt the need to be competitive, and simply do not have the customer focus that a competitive company needs.

Owning the market

What companies must ask themselves is whether real profits can be generated by following the lead set by others – or whether it may not be more profitable to create a new market segment altogether.

In this day of intensive competition, few companies will ever enjoy the luxurious position of owning the market, or see their brand become synonymous with a product. True, there are market leaders – for rental cars, Hertz; for hamburgers, McDonald's; for ketchup, Heinz; for instant photographs, Polaroid. Yet companies such as Coca-Cola, Hoover and Xerox are the exceptions. Most companies will be forced to compete in a market in which there are a variety of players. In such a case, it is not enough to offer 'more of the same'. Instead, success depends on offering 'more of something different'.

The world of pizzas gives very good examples of this narrowing focus. In the US, for many years Pizza Hut 'owned' the market. New companies wishing to eat into Pizza Hut's pizza had to focus on specific parts of the business. Today, Little Caesars is number two in the category, and has gained this position by concentrating on the take-away business. Number three, Domino's Pizza, has focused on another part of the business, that of home delivery. So both Little Caesars and Domino's Pizza were able to carve out a successful chunk of the total pizza business by focusing very clearly, very precisely, on a narrow area, and then going for it for all they were worth.

Another example of concentrating on a specific area in a market can be found in the service sector. When Federal Express entered the market with its unique hub-and-spoke operation, few observers gave it much of a chance. But then Federal Express decided to focus very clearly on one aspect of the business, overnight delivery. The rest is, of course, history.

In each of these examples, success has been found by isolating an aspect of the business that is not yet sufficiently served by the competition. This requires deep knowledge – not just of the competition, but also, more specifically, of the consumer, and of the *needs* of the consumer.

Anger and intolerance are the twin enemies of correct understanding.
                                                    – Mahatma Gandhi

Know the market

While Procter & Gamble were concentrating on Unilever, Unilever were concentrating on the market. It discovered that black women in Brazil did not have a shampoo suitable for their particular type of hair. Introducing Afro hair products developed for other countries was not an option, as the Brazilian climate was different and products reacted to the climate in an unacceptable way. Researchers of the Gessy Lever cosmetics division spent more than two years developing the SedaKeraforce shampoo brand for Brazilian black women. 'The four products contain extracts from the plant keroba, which is native to the Amazonian forest. Brazil's Afro hair care market has annual sales of $160 million.'[10]

Whirlpool, one of the world's leading manufacturers of white-good appliances, also took the needs of its (potential) customers into account when they developed a new washing machine specifically for the Indian market. The company's researchers discovered that Indians particularly like purity and hygiene. These qualities are associated in their minds with white. But there has always been a problem about washing white garments. The local water discolours white clothes after a number of washes, and this is seen as a considerable drawback to owning automatic washing machines. In response Whirlpool custom-designed an automatic machine that was particularly good with white fabrics:

> Whirlpool hasn't stopped there. It uses generous incentives to get thousands of Indian retailers to stock its goods. To reach every cranny of the vast nation, it uses local contractors conversant in India's eighteen languages to collect payments in cash and deliver appliances by truck, bicycles, even oxcart. Since 1996, Whirlpool's sales in India have leapt 80 per cent – and should hit $200 million this year. Whirlpool now is the leading brand in India's fast-growing market for fully automatic washing machines.[11]

And finally, here is another example of giving consumers what they want: a free newspaper.

> Metro, the free newspaper has become a hit among young urban, mobile commuters – a segment of the population that traditional newspapers had largely lost to the internet and TV. Metro International now has thirty city editions – including twelve in the Netherlands alone – in fourteen countries in Europe, North America and South America. With a combined daily circulation

*topping 3 million and an estimated readership of 6.6 million,
Metro, according to Stockholm-based international investment group
Carnegie, is the world's fifth most-read newspaper brand. 'At first,
Metro was given a hard time by the agencies,'* [Mainardo de
Nardis, CEO of the CIA Group, which owns Metro] *said.
'They thought that if it isn't paid for, it has less appeal – and was
not read by choice. All that has proved to be totally untrue.' Also,
the concept of placing the papers free on Metro-branded racks in
subways and other busy commuter points, such as nearby retail
outlets and fast-food restaurants, is proving a hit with advertisers.'*[12]

When the going gets tough

Nobody is suggesting that it is easy to be competitive in today's
ultra-fast world. All too often, companies are forced to evaluate a
market lead in terms of weeks rather than years. Yet, despite all
this, the traditional success factors of business – getting to the
market first, becoming market leader, initiating rather than following and innovating rather than copying – still hold fast.

The three examples quoted above show companies concentrating on the market rather than on the competition. All three work
at identifying market needs, and then building a strategy to satisfy
those needs.

But creating a competitive advantage today raises considerable
problems for companies that have become sluggish, overfed and
unresponsive. There is a depressing lack of agility in both companies and management. The windows of opportunity open for just a
fleeting, brief moment. It takes managers who are concentrating on
opportunity – rather than focusing single-mindedly on attacking

the competition – to see the potential of such chances. They do not occur frequently. They do not occur with any predictability. But when they do, managers and organisations that are not fettered by bureaucracy, by long lines of authority and decision-making, are best placed to take advantage of them.

Towards a business eco-system?

In today's competitive world, companies are more interlinked than ever before. There is a growing conviction that we can no longer place companies into hermetically sealed units, able to continue regardless of what is happening elsewhere. And for this reason, some experts are discussing the emergence of a Business Eco-System, in which the inter-relationships between companies are more fully understood. In their book *The Soul at Work*, authors Roger Lewin and Birute Regine state:

> *It is possible to think of any Business Eco-System in terms of a network of companies, each occupying a place in its own landscape of possibilities; and each landscape being coupled to many others: those of competitors, collaborators and complementors. As the landscape of one of the companies changes – perhaps through a leapfrogging innovation – the landscapes of those connected to it will also change: some will increase in size, while others get smaller, or even disappear.[13]*

The objective of the traditional corporation is to manage one or more operating business units so that they grow revenues and profits, and so that they live long. This form of organisation focuses managers' attention on two things: their core markets and their core operations. According to another expert, James Moore the problem with this model is that it creates in managers a corresponding blindness to developments occurring outside their core.[14] That is, the 'white space' between existing markets and operations is left, to a large extent, unattended. Yet, in a global economy with ample free capital, talented knowledge partners, and technological inventiveness, much of the opportunity facing businesses originates in the white space. This is true whether one is seeking to extend one's existing business – or develop new ones.

For Lewin and Regine, the benefits include 'the opportunity to reap great rewards through the economics of increasing returns and through forming alliances or other forms of partnerships. But when everything is connected directly or indirectly to everything else, changes in one part of the system may be propagated throughout the web of connections, and sometimes organisations become extinct through no fault of their own.'[15]

> *Beware the fury of a patient man.*
>
> – John Dryden

Don't fight them – join them

Concentrating on competition – we'll beat them to it! – greatly reduces the chances for creating opportunities. Competition can lead to exclusion. And exclusion can lead to a loss of competitiveness. Constant attack is a not the only method of creating a competitive edge. Alliances often provide a greater opportunity for win–win situations. And any action which can turn a potential

friend into a permanent enemy could have far-reaching consequences of an even catastrophic nature.

Companies must learn to operate with more inner confidence.
They must not attack for fear of being side-tracked. They must not
attack because 'that's the way we have always done things'. They
must learn to open their minds to the market and create the ability
to harness a company's potential instantly. It means having things
in place *before* they are needed, rather than constantly watching the
competition to find out what is needed next. For by adopting a
wait-and-see attitude, companies can all too easily miss the brief
window of opportunity as it opens, with the result that they will
inevitably be forced into following the market – and never lead it.

We are not saying that you should turn a blind eye to the competition. We are not saying that you should stop gaining insight
into the competitors' plans or stop keeping up with their latest features and designs. We are not saying you should abandon pre-emptive strikes to safeguard your market position.

What we are saying is that too many companies today are prepared to pick up the crumbs from the leaders' tables. They are prepared to let others do the hard work, make the breakthroughs,
create world-impacting technologies and products, and then hope
to pick up some profit by doing something derivative and conven-
tional.

Attacking the competition has taken the place of mobilising
your own resources. And when this happens, it becomes a deadly
sin.

CASES

The sinner: Infineon

For many years, the chip industry seemed to offer a licence to print money: in 2000, it booked a record year, with a growth of 89 per cent. Yet the resulting dramatic downturn in the market – in 2001 sales plummeted by 32 per cent, causing major producers to cut capital expenditure as factories ran at about half their capacity – brought to light a fatal flaw in the industry: it spends too much time copying competitors and not enough time listening to customers and creating market developments.

On 1 April 1999 Siemens Semiconductors transformed itself into Infineon Technologies, a younger, dynamic, more flexible company geared towards success in the competitive, ever-changing world of microelectronics. Infineon Technologies' IPO in March 2000 was Germany's second largest stock-market flotation; within hours of the opening of trading, shares in Infineon Technologies doubled in value. The issue had been oversubscribed thirty-three times. In 2001, the company's revenues were €5.67 billion, and this placed Infineon firmly in the world's top ten semiconductor companies; it was also the world's fourth largest producer of computer memory chips. Yet it could not avoid the downturn in the market: within one year, Infineon was battered by the dramatic slowdown in global chip demand from computer and phone makers and particularly hard hit as prices for dynamic random-access memory chips sank well below the cost of producing them. To bolster its finances, Infineon announced cost-cutting measures and a hiring freeze in its battle against falling demand. In addition, it cut 5,000 jobs in a restructuring plan aimed at saving €1 billion during 2001–2.

For many years, semiconductor companies have been fighting a civil war: they have boosted capacity (the 'mine-is-bigger-than-yours' syndrome) and pushed new chip development with only one thing in mind: to beat the competition. And in all this, they have forgotten one thing: the needs of the customers.

Infineon Technologies launched itself as a flexible, dynamic company; it proved itself as blinkered and competition-focused as all the other players in the market. And this – ultimately – caused its failure.

The saint: Dyson

Let's face it, one vacuum cleaner is very much like another. And the major brands all offered virtually the same features: higher suction power, disposable bags, long lead, swivel wheels, accessories that ended up in the cupboard under the stairs, and a wonderful range of colours. Any changes to the product were largely cosmetic; incremental improvements aimed at doing little more than keeping up with the competitors.

Until Dyson entered the market.

James Dyson came up with his idea for a revolutionary vacuum cleaner in 1978. He was renovating his country home when he became frustrated at the way his vacuum cleaner's dust bag became clogged up – with the consequential loss of suction power. Five years – and 5,127 prototypes – later he created the bagless vacuum cleaner. Two more years were spent trying to find a manufacturer who would produce the new product under licence, and after all attempts in Europe had failed, Dyson finally decided to try Japan. In 1986, the Dyson vacuum cleaner was launched on the Japanese market where it achieved something approaching cult status – and sold for $2,000. In 1991, it was awarded the International Design Fair prize in Japan, and today Dyson products are on display at museums across the world, including the Victoria & Albert Museum in London, the San Francisco Museum of Modern Art, the Georges Pompidou Centre in Paris and the Powerhouse Museum in Sydney.

Using income from the Japanese licence, Dyson decided to manufacture a new model under his own name in the UK; he opened his own research facility and factory in 1993. There he developed the DCO1, based on the patented 'dual cyclone' technology. The costs of patenting this new technology were so large that the company was almost forced into bankruptcy; by 1995, however, the DCO1 accounted for more than 50 per cent of sales in the UK market. Hoover, until then its undisputed leader, saw its market share plummet from more than 25 per cent to less than 10 per cent.

Dyson continued its policy of innovation-based development, and introduced a full range of cleaners on to the market. Hoover, however, locked in the old mindset, introduced, in 1999, its own bagless vacuum cleaner. Dyson took the matter to the High Court, where it was decided that Hoover had copied the Dyson technology. In his verdict the judge pointed out that until Dyson had patented its bagless technology, the thought of developing such a technology had been anathema within an industry that earned ongoing profits from the sale of vacuum-cleaner bags. Commenting on the verdict, James Dyson remarked, 'Why on earth don't they [Hoover] think of their own ideas instead of copying ours?'[16]

The Third Deadly Sin

Sloth in Executive Decisions

Focus on the future – and let the present take care of itself

You've reached the top and now you work day and night to keep those pretenders to the throne at bay. You recognise your true obligation: to keep people focused on the future, to direct their minds to strategy, to thinking ahead. And day-to-day decisions? Well, you've got your subordinates to look after those. They don't require your talents. You must look ahead. Stare into the future. Tell people about how the future will shape up and bring you enormous prosperity. You're a man of vision. The work can be done by others ...

Sin-O-Meter for Sloth

The deadly sin of sloth? You? You work all hours and still people accuse you of being lazy. But how right are they? Answer these questions and discover whether you are taking the easy way out.

1 You are asked in an interview to discuss your company's course. Do you: a) boast that your company will be market leader in five years; b) point out that long-term projections simply don't count in your volatile market; c) announce a new development alliance with a leading competitor?

2 Your internal communications department develops a series of posters. Do you choose: a) The future belongs to us; b) Success is today's satisfied customer; c) Growth is our number one priority?

3 You are asked to name your most important management quality. Do you choose: a) vision; b) your ability to make incredibly motivating (and amusing) speeches; c) a determination to understand customers?

4 You are developing a business plan for your company. Is your major priority: a) growth; b) flexibility; c) as much profit as you can squeeze out of the company?

5 You have to deliver a speech at the annual company party. Do you: a) concentrate on the big picture; b) phone that writer you met the other week in the bar and get her to put something down on paper for you; c) tell your colleagues that times are going to be hard, so the name of the game will be change?

6 A headhunter approaches you with an interesting career opportunity. Do you: a) ask for detailed information about the company's current position; b) demand total freedom to implement

some far-reaching plans; c) ask for projections about future prof-itability?

7 Your company is suffering losses. Do you: a) announce that this is incidental and future profits are now sure to be higher than initially calculated; b) tell your accounting department to come up with some way to create a better picture; c) set up a think-tank to analyse your strengths and market opportunities?

8 You are faced with a changing market for your services. Do you: a) open an internet site with Flash (of course); b) write a new five-year business plan; c) tell everybody that the market has got it wrong and things will pick up in no time?

9 A division within your company is underperforming, even though the market seems to be buoyant. Do you: a) set targets for the division; b) put it on the market; c) fire the director?

10 The shareholders call an extraordinary general meeting to air criticism about the way you are handling the business. Do you: a) resign and demand a high severance handshake; b) show them projections that prove you are going to make important profits within the next three years; c) show them up-to-date figures concerning time-to-market and greater flexibility throughout the company?

Scores

1 a) 6; b) 2; c) 1
2 a) 5; b) 2; c) 5
3 a) 6; b) 8; c) 1
4 a) 3; b) 1; c) 5
5 a) 2; b) 3; c) 6
6 a) 1; b) 4; c) 5
7 a) 4; b) 11; c) 2
8 a) 4; b) 5; c) 6
9 a) 2; b) 4; c) 9
10 a) 6; b) 8; c) 2

0 ══════════════════════════ 80

Where are you on the scale? The farther you are to the right, the lazier you are!

The past is gone, and cannot be changed. The present is the result of decisions made in the past, and therefore can only be experienced. The future is there for us to create. We are the masters of our own destiny. We can do anything. We can turn the future into anything we want it to be. We are the champions. We're simply the best!

What greater challenge than to create a new, unique future? It is a challenge that is eagerly accepted by managers keen to make an impact on their company's prosperity. And so, increasingly, managers focus on the future. Developing plans for new markets, new products, new customers, new profits. Designing strategies to take their companies into an ever more prosperous spiral of growth.

The future is out there; we can grasp it and make it our own.

The future has a powerful attraction for anybody in business. Growth, continuity, expansion – these are all matters that occupy the minds of managers. Creating strategies aimed at future success is a core aspect of a manager's job. Certainly, the appearance of such milestone books as *Future Shock*[1] and more recently *Competing for the Future*[2] has contributed to the realisation that things are not going to be what they have always been. Armed with the conviction that change is essential if future success is to be guaranteed, many managers have decided that their primary task is to change course and steer their companies towards new oceans where the catch can be enormous.

The future beckons; it is there for the taking by the brave.

And the brave – as well as the headstrong – rush to stake their claim in the future.

> *The future is something which everyone reaches at the rate of*
> *60 minutes an hour, whatever he does, whoever he be.*
> – C. S. Lewis

On the divide

Today we are still on the divide between the Industrial Economy and the Knowledge-based Economy. Such a divide always creates its own difficulties. We saw this during the last great paradigm shift, as we moved from the Agricultural Economy into the Industrial Economy.

The worldwide Agricultural Economy peaked in 1890, when farmers, hunters, foresters and fishermen produced close to 30 per cent of Gross National Product. As the Industrial Economy began to bite, so the percentage of GNP produced by the agricultural sector declined, replaced by industries such as manufacturing, construction and public utilities. In the 1970s, these industries enjoyed phenomenal success, but by the 1990s – as the Knowledge-based Economy started to supersede the Industrial Economy – they began to decline, and were responsible for just slightly more than 35 per cent of GNP. By this time, incidentally, agriculture was responsible for only a mere 8 per cent of GNP.

And so we can see that, just as industry rose to supersede agriculture, so services are emerging to take over in importance from industry. Communications, trade, finance – these are some of the services which now, with 57 per cent of GNP, are leading world economic growth.[3]

It is understandable, then, that managers of industry-based companies – or those with their roots in such companies – should constantly be looking for ways of moving into areas most likely to expand in the Knowledge-based Economy. This is where future profits are to be found; this is where sustainability can be achieved.

'Let me show you the future'

Long-term strategies are based on predictions. It has always been the case, and nothing today has changed this. Markets are 'expected' to develop in this way; consumers are 'expected' to demand such and such; investments are 'expected' to start earning returns; R&D efforts are 'expected' to result in new products and technologies.

Expectations, however, are always high. Always positive. Few managers will ever say that the 'expectations' are for the company to go into decline.

In July 1999, Compaq announced a daring new strategy:

The world's largest personal computer maker, Compaq, is to emulate some of its fast-growing rivals by increasing sales direct to the public. Traditionally it has sold its PCs through dealers and retailers, but it is to step up its direct sales as it defends its market-leading position, said new chief executive Michael Capellas. 'With this appointment, Compaq now has in place everything necessary to be at the forefront of the accelerating revolution in information technology,' said company chairman Benjamin Rosen. 'Michael Capellas will lead the company through the next and greatest phase of its growth.' The veteran computer executive and technology consultant with a background in the energy exploration industry said the company aimed to rapidly grow sales of its PCs direct to customers, as its fast-growing rivals do, rather than through dealers. 'Today, our direct PC sales are at 15 per cent. By the end of the year, we will be at 25 per cent. On a going-forward model, we want to be at 40 per cent,' he said.[4]

It was a daring strategy, fully justified by the predictions produced by the company. Their figures all seemed to add up. The expectations were high. The investors applauded. Compaq's share price increased. Success was guaranteed.

Compaq's future had never been brighter. But almost exactly two years later the following news hit the headlines:

> *Earlier this month, Compaq sent a tremor through the stock markets after cutting its sales forecasts and axing a further 4,000 workers. Profits at the world's second largest personal computer maker fell to $67 million compared to $338 million in the same period a year ago. Including a special restructuring charge of $439 million, the firm ran up losses of $279 million during the three months. A slowdown-provoked slump in demand has been the root of the computer maker's troubles; however, Compaq's troubles cannot solely be attributed to the slowdown. Its rival Dell has steadily been gaining market share, overtaking Compaq as the world's most popular personal computer maker earlier this year. Compaq also stressed that it would retreat from the front line of PC sales after suffering from intense price competition from Dell. Compaq now plans to refocus its business on software and computer services. 'In the short-term, the market remains volatile and thus difficult to predict with much certainty,' said the company's chief executive and chairman Michael Capellas.'5*

It had taken just two years for reality to overtake expectations. Not only had the market developed and reacted differently to expectations, Compaq had also lost its position as the world's leading PC manufacturer and had fallen back to number two.

Do not count on much from the future,
nor trouble your mind about the past.

– Chinese proverb

Growth, growth, growth

If a company records growth in forty straight quarters, then you can assume that it will continue indefinitely. Right?

Wrong!

Cisco Systems had developed a sophisticated IT system that allowed managers to track supply and demand in 'real time'. This also allowed them to make 'pinpoint' forecasts. But nobody had ever taken into account the fact that growth could disappear. Forty straight quarters of growth had made that assumption seem ludicrous. Even as evidence to the contrary began to pile up, the assumption of growth could not be shaken. In December 2000, despite all the evidence of a market slowdown, CEO John Chambers forecasted a 50 per cent annual growth and declared, 'I have never been more optimistic about the future of our industry as a whole or of Cisco.'

In April 2001, declining sales forced Cisco to write down $2.5 billion in excess inventory and lay off 8,500 employees. Its shares lost 88 per cent of their value in just one year.[6]

The future is the worst thing about the present.

– Gustave Flaubert

Preaching hope

Today's managers have become adept at painting a picture of prosperity waiting just round the corner. Perhaps all too adept. They focus on the future to the cost of everything else. Or rather, they concentrate on futures, always ready with a new future when the one they predicted either does not arrive or arrives in a guise they had not foreseen. It doesn't seem to matter whether the future brings prosperity; rather, the hope that it will seems to be sufficient justification for most managers.

They have adopted the practice of preaching hope. We can 'hope' for continued success; we can 'hope' the market will continue to develop as predicted; we can 'hope' to achieve a strong position with our new product range.

Hope is one of the three great virtues; managers who preach hope are preaching virtue.

But they're also preaching indifference to the present. They preach that our existing business – the one based on our proven competencies – will look after itself while they concentrate on the future. Today is irrelevant; tomorrow counts.

Let us create the future!

Locked in or locked out?

Promoting expectations, preaching hope, building ever-new strategies – all these add up to an attempt to grasp the ungraspable. It is understandable that managers should wish to secure a prosperous future for their companies. Yet we seriously wonder whether this is best done by focusing on the future and allowing the present to take care of itself.

All too often, decisions taken about the future lock a company into a specific direction. Focusing on the future demands a particular sort of single-minded dedication. There is little room left for manoeuvre. It implies rejecting options, alternatives. A company can find itself locked into a strategy – and locked out of the market that could have produced profits.

It has created a future for itself – but finds it is locked in that future all on its own.

Such a situation frequently arises when managers concentrate on external matters – the market – rather than concentrating on developing internal strengths. In other words, managers prefer to predict what others will do, rather than taking steps themselves to create a company that is resilient to change – a company that is flexible enough to be adaptable to new situations and to take advantage of emerging opportunities *as they occur*.

The future happens whether we like it or not. Successful managers build in an ability to react to the future as soon as it happens.

Concentrating on the business of business

In 1999, British Airways, the 'world's favourite' and for many years most profitable airline, announced a major switch in its market focus. In a televised broadcast CEO Robert Ayling declared that the airline's strategy was now switching and would concentrate on business travel at the expense of the cut-throat economy travel market, adding: 'This will ensure that we stay ahead while reducing our exposure to the heavily discounted element of the economy sector.' Analysts in the City of London welcomed the overhaul of company strategy, believing that the company was putting in place the right strategy to fight off the sharp decline in its profits. The airline's strategy for recovery focused on updating its long-haul fleet, introducing more Boeing 777 aircraft, smaller than 747s but containing fewer economy seats. 'The introduction of new premium products is key for British Airways. It is the catalyst that will help them regain their premier airline status,' said Chris Tarry, airline analyst with Commerzbank.[7]

Ayling left BA early in 2000, but the airline stuck to its strategy of increasing the number of highly profitable business-class passengers at the expense of its economy-class business, in spite of making that year its worst set of results since it had been privatised seventeen years before. BA also had to respond to the new, low-cost airlines and international alliances that were threatening its traditional business. In Europe, it did this by setting up its own low-cost subsidiary, Go; Go was later acquired by a group of venture capitalists and in May 2002, it was sold to its highly successful competitor EasyJet. Low-budget airlines such as EasyJet and Ryanair have consistently outperformed BA, pushing them down the list of preferred British airlines. Mr O'Leary, who was responsible for the relaunch of Ryanair when it was on the point of crash-landing ten years ago and took its inspiration from the success of Southwest Airlines in the United States, said it had 'never been easier' for companies like Ryanair to expand into Europe, because the bigger players, especially BA, SAS and Alitalia, were abandoning routes.

The unpredictable

Nobody in business – or anywhere else, for that matter – could possibly have foreseen the events of 11 September 2001. In just forty-five minutes, the world changed for ever. What followed was an unpredicted and unpredictable global collapse of the aviation industry. In just eight weeks some 250,000 jobs were lost. Sabena, one of the world's oldest airlines, filed for bankruptcy. Swissair was another casualty. Aircraft were mothballed. Redundancies hit not only the airlines but also suppliers, catering companies, airline builders, engine manufacturers, travel agencies, and even bus and taxi companies that focused on airport transportation.

British Airways suffered badly. The strategy they had adopted – concentrating on the profitable business traveller – made them less flexible. Business travel was hit very hard, cutting very deep into operational returns and turning predicted profits into the highest losses ever seen in the airline industry.

Of course, many analysts are now saying that a restructuring of the industry had in fact been inevitable. There were simply too many airlines offering too many seats to too few passengers. In the resulting game of musical chairs airlines, anxious to survive, are seeking alliances with other players. The days of national flag-carriers seem numbered. In Europe, people are predicting (that word again) that ultimately there could just remain three major airlines – or combination of airlines. Despite its malaise at the moment, BA is still considered one of the potential 'Big Three', possibly in alliance with KLM or even other major carriers.

Anyone prepared to take bets on the ultimate outcome?

These things are in the future; we needs must do what lies at hand.

– Sophocles

A new scapegoat?

Does this mean that managers will now use the events of 11 September to rethink radically their ideas or will 11 September simply serve to justify their past inaccuracies? Certainly, the chance is great that what happened in America and the resulting crises in Afghanistan and Iraq will be mentioned as contributory causes of failure in company reports for many years to come. We can expect statements such as 'We were on track to improved profits until ...' and 'The unexpected events of ...' and 'We have readjusted our growth predictions in light of the events of ...' and 'The erosion of our market share is directly related to the events of ...' and 'We are confident of an upturn in our results, after the inevitable dip following the events of ...'

It isn't often that managers are offered such a scapegoat! And there is a danger – a very real danger – that they will seize on this and use the insecurity the events engendered to justify their continuing in the same way as ever.

Yet one lesson we can learn from 11 September – although it seems callous to speak of business lessons in this context – is that in business, as in life, we do not create the future – we can do little more than participate in it. No predictions, no projections can take account of the unpredictable. And for this very reason, we must not focus on the future, but rather on creating today a mindset that is able to switch tracks as events demand. In a time when there is simply not enough time, when life-cycles are counted in weeks rather than years, when opportunities appear and disappear overnight, we cannot focus on the future. We cannot allow ourselves to create an illusion when we are actually in the business of reality.

Creating the future means creating the ability to seize opportunities as they occur, not predicting whether they will happen or not.

> *From passions grow opinions;*
> *intellectual laziness lets these harden into convictions.*
> — Friedrich Nietzsche

Join the future

In May 1999, the BBC reported the following: 'The head of the largest maker of computer chips in the world has predicted that companies which fail to establish a presence on the internet will go out of business within five years. "In five years, there won't be any internet companies because they will all be *internet* companies," said Andrew Grove, chairman of Intel. "Otherwise they will die."'[8]

Today, many people wonder whether the dot.com bubble has truly burst. Certainly, many companies have come to realise that the internet is not the magic potion that many said it would be. The internet is not taking over the world. Shops and department stores are not closing down as consumers switch *en masse* to doing all their shopping online. Yet for many years, the internet prophets – often with vested interests in the expansion of the technology – tried to force their view of the future on to the world. Many managers were determined not to be left behind, and jumped on the bandwagon.

Let's get our hands on the internet pot of gold.

All that glitters is not gold. But some people can create the illusion of gold as long as there are enough fools around. Investors were eager to pour their money into companies that predicted future growth and unparalleled future opportunities. Share prices of dot.com companies soared. Suddenly, eager young entrepreneurs – at least those who were the most convincing – found themselves millionaires overnight. Not because of any work they had done, but simply because, like some modern-day medicine-men, they had convinced people to believe in an illusion. They showed people their vision of the future, and those people wanted – no matter what it cost – to be included in it.

Never underestimate the power of greed.

Things, however, took a different turn, and soon those same investors began to question the earning capacity of many dot.com companies. Were shares in such companies really worth what they had made them worth? After all, very few companies were posting anything more than promises.

Was it inevitable?

In retrospect, it is perhaps inevitable that the bubble should have burst. Long-term promises of future prosperity have a limited sell-by date. Ultimately, promise has to be matched by performance. When it doesn't, the market grows cold; impatience does not make for a healthy climate.

The climate grows positively hostile when the casualties begin falling. And there were casualties enough. 'The sharp declines in the internet advertising market convinced us that it didn't make sense to pursue a portal strategy,' said chief financial officer Mark

Begor, when US broadcasting giant NBC axed NBCi, its loss-making internet subsidiary. 'We wanted to find a way to maximise sharcholder value and wind down the business in the best way possible.' While NBCi chief executive Will Lansing commented, 'Rather than continuing to operate at a significant loss, and having the value of NBCi continue to erode, we believe this transaction is in the best interest of NBCi's public stockholders.'[9]

> *I don't try to describe the future. I try to prevent it.*
>
> – Ray Bradbury

Those unreliable consumers

Part of this meltdown was due to consumers not doing what, in surveys, they had said they would do. How terribly unreliable of them! Yet it seems flying in the face of reality to place such importance on stated consumer trends. It is one thing for consumers to say they would buy things on the internet, and quite another for them to act on this once they have been confronted with reports that credit card details may not be as secure as they have been told. While it was very easy for customers to click and buy, many became frustrated by the long wait they then had to endure before the product arrived. In the click-and-go economy, immediate (at lcast very prompt) delivery was the minimum expectation. And clearly, many companies had somehow overlooked the need for a well-oiled distribution machine that would switch into gear immediately. They thought that the deal was everything.

But the biggest casualties of too much focus on the future are undoubtedly the telecom companies. Projections for ownership of mobile phones showed an almost unbelievable rise. In 1998, Hein van der Zeeuw, then marketing manager of the GSM division of Philips Semiconductors, addressed the world's IC industry at the annual ISS Conference. In his keynote speech he sketched this picture of the industry:

> *The growth of cellphone users has been faster than anybody predicted. Today there are around 250 million subscribers in the world; by the year 2000, that figure will have risen to around 600 million subscribers. At least if the growth continues in the way it has over the past five years. Up to now it has followed an exponential curve and we have no reason to assume that this growth rate will change in the foreseeable future. We could even be in for a surprise – and be faced with faster growth. But whatever the actual figure will ultimately be, one thing is sure: it'll be BIG. Really BIG. And when you think that the market is only a few years old, then the present penetration of portable cellular phones is nothing less than phenomenal. To put this growth into an even greater perspective: do you realise it took well over half a century for the normal telephone to reach a high level of penetration? I bet there are even some people in this room who, like me, can remember living in a house without a telephone. The penetration rate for cellular phones has been reached in just half a decade! Last year, the industry produced 140 million cellular phones; this year it will produce an estimated 180 million. Do you realise that we now produce more cellular phones annually than we do televisions? More than automobiles?[10]*

It was a market that seemed to give people in the industry an excuse to print money. And many people were convinced that this area would be the one that provided the adhesive between the consumer and the internet. The companies were eager to outdo the competition, and when the licences came up for sale, there was a bidding frenzy the like of which has rarely been witnessed.

Another one bites the dust

Now the whole industry is in shambles. Investments have been so enormous that people wonder whether they can ever be recouped. Certainly, the *Financial Times* has serious doubts about the whole industry – both its past and its future.

The bidding for 3G mobile licences marked the turning point in an investment frenzy that sucked in $4,000 billion. At the height of the boom, mobile phone operators felt they had hit upon a formula that guaranteed success. They could point to rapidly increasing usage, helped by heavy handset subsidies and design improvements. Then there was the potential of the internet to increase revenues by offering mass-market consumers media content and shopping online. Yet almost from the moment those cheques were written at the 3G licence auction in the UK, the industry has foundered. After a similar auction in Germany raised even more money a few weeks later, the whole European telecom industry was groaning under levels of debt that made banking regulators wonder whether the financial markets could cope with the strain. Today, the projections the mobile phone operators used to justify investing so much money look increasingly spurious. Technical snags mean that no manufacturer has yet demonstrated commercial equipment operating at anything close to the promised data speeds. One of the most influential regular studies of mobile *phone use, produced by A. T. Kearney management consultants and Cambridge Business School, is due to reveal that most consumers are utterly uninterested in surfing the internet from their mobile phone. Of 2,400 mobile phone users interviewed, just 4 per cent said they thought they were ever likely to use their phone to spend money online (down from 12 per cent in the last survey, six months ago). Only 2 per cent had tried to do this with existing generations of internet-enabled phones, which have already cost the industry hundreds of millions of dollars to deploy. The investment stampede was made possible by an explosion in cheap debt financing not seen since the junk bond craze of the 1980s. Venture capital companies, whose coffers had swollen once the investing public saw the potential of the internet, began queuing up to pump in private equity money before taking fledgeling companies public. That might have been that, but for a twist that lifted the telecom bubble out of the class of the investment booms that had swept through the dot.com and biotech industries. This twist was the late arrival of established companies with balance sheets and credit ratings solid enough to borrow tens of billions of dollars. Some were manufacturing giants such as Britain's GEC, which turned itself inside out to focus on a telecom equipment division renamed Marconi. Others such as Scottish Power, National Grid, Enron and Montana Power were utility companies that spotted an opportunity to make use of their infrastructure skills but had no experience in telecom. The most dangerous were the traditional telephone companies, which were trying to prove they were no longer the dull monopolies of old. Each of the three largest had a new chief executive fresh from the computing industry and anxious to spend money. Mike Armstrong jumped from International Business Machines to AT&T, Sir Peter Bonfield went from ICL to BT and Ron Sommer arrived from Sony to run a privatised Deutsche Telekom. All these companies, incumbents and start-ups alike, believed they could find additional sources of revenue to justify their investment, either then or in the future. In retrospect, this was always far-fetched. The proliferation of distinct access technologies meant a typical household or small business was being offered telephone and internet services by as many as a dozen networks, all dependent on growing market share.'[11]*

The sad truth

There is still no such thing as a sure bet. No matter what any entrepreneur may tell you. And there is no safe bet on the future. By focusing on the future, many companies have allowed their current business to go wanting.

Ultimately, focusing exclusively on the future is totally alien to good business practice. Traditionally, a company's value was based on its actual results; by constantly focusing on the future, results are pushed into the background and are replaced with promises. The future horizons many managers suggest totally ignore the past – and with it the proven competencies of a company – in order to create a possible future that has no links with a company's strengths. In addition, it locks the company on to a course that may be relevant now, but may no longer be so in a short time. As life-cycles shrink and new opportunities present themselves at a moment's notice – often without any prior warning – concentrating on a future decided yesterday may be concentrating on something that will never happen. What's more, the managers who continually look to the future are often confusing: today it is this future, tomorrow it is a different one altogether. Those who preach hope do so with an ulterior motive. Hope is used to disguise a threat: jump on the bandwagon or leave. And managers who focus on the promises of the future try desperately to create that future even if it is alien to the one that would evolve if their companies were true to their roots.

Sloth, not ill-will, makes me unjust.

– Mason Cooley

Operating in Zero Time

Future health is not found by focusing on the future. There are no reliable predictions, certainly, in a time and market when things can change overnight. What companies must learn is that the future happens, and they must equip themselves to operate flexibly, efficiently and, most importantly, instantly. They must learn to operate in Zero Time, recognising that it is better to be fast to a market than to predict a market that never materialises.

There is an old Russian saying: '"So," said the poor man, "I would drink vodka, but I have no money".' You get the feeling today that many managers focusing on the future are already drinking vodka by the bucketful. Having no money – or rather, having nothing more than the prospect of unimaginable fortunes in the future – does not seem to bother them. Nor does it seem to bother the many investors who are all too eager to pick up the tab for a bottle of vodka in the hope of eventually owning the distillery – investors who are prepared to accept the promises and eagerly buy shares in the future.

Nothing is easier than to be correct after the event. To be right in retrospect. But history shows us that the future is a force unto itself. Predictions are little more than that. Even Nostradamus did not get it right all of the time.

We may attempt to create the future. But the future has a way of creating itself. And it is all too often a future that we could never have imagined.

Do not allow yourself to be wooed by the future. It will happen, no matter what you do. Do not waste time trying to predict the way consumers will act. Instead, concentrate on creating a company that is agile, adaptable, flexible and swift. For it is these qualities that will help you to understand and grasp the future sooner than your rivals.

And if you decide that the future is the safest place to be? Well, then you will surely suffer the consequences of the deadly sin of sloth.

CASES

The sinner: KPNQwest

It is the biggest and most important fibre-optics network in Europe, and the backbone of the internet throughout the continent, yet its owner, KPNQwest, has filed for bankruptcy and has seen its value drop from €42 billion in 2000 to just €5 million in 2002.

KPNQwest was formed in 1998 by KPN, the Dutch telecom giant, and Kwest in the United States. It immediately embarked on an ambitious policy of building and contracting telecommunications networks across Europe. By 2001, just over two years later, it had sales of over €850 million and it had connected more than fifty major European cities to its fibre-optics network, which now measured 20,000 kilometres. And it was still expanding, investing and acquiring even more capacity: in 2001 it bought the British provider GTS Bone for €650 million even though this increased its debt to €1.9 billion – still believing its own optimistic forecasts and assuming that heavy losses in this industry only served to pave the way to long-standing profits. And so it continued to build communications capacity in an area that already had too much of it, rather than concentrating on improving sales and profit margins.

Even the danger signs, which started flashing in fluorescent lights, didn't deter the company from believing in its growth-driven strategy – a behaviour nothing short of corporate stubbornness, for the warnings were coming from its parent company KPN.

During 2001, KPN had desperately been trying to dig its way out of a situation of its own making. By September 2001, its debts had grown to €23 billion, its planned merger with Belgium Telecom had failed, and staff were being laid off. It ended 2001 with the largest loss of any company in corporate Dutch history. And owing KPNQwest €23 million.

In February 2002, KPNQwest issued a statement saying that it had sufficient cash to continue its operations; by mid May, however, it said that credit protection was not an option, and by the end of the month it was advising companies to look elsewhere for capacity. It filed for bankruptcy on 31 May 2002. A concerted effort has been made to keep the network open, but the KPNQwest story is likely to finish in a manner familiar to telecom investors: the only people likely to make back any money are the banks and lenders, leaving bondholders and equity investors out in the cold.

The saint: Bertelsmann

In a time when media companies – ITV Digital, Kirch – are filing for bankruptcy, Bertelsmann appears to be flying in the face of adversity, and booking high profits and increased shareholder dividends. It announced in March 2002 that it wass expecting to top the record earnings of the year 2000–2001.

According to chairman and CEO Thomas Middelhof,

Bertelsmann is the most international of media corporations, striving to be the world's leader in the markets in which it operates. We provide customers with information, education and entertainment through every possible outlet and in every conceivable format. Our efforts focus on creative content, customer relations and strong return on capital. Bertelsmann is a renowned home for talent, giving artists and entrepreneurs room to grow. As the world of media rapidly changes, we are at the cutting edge.[12]

So why has Bertelsmann been able to avoid going the way of so many other media and internet companies?

The answer can perhaps be found in its use of the Bertelsmann Excellence Initiative (BEX), which involves a strategic employment of capital gains from the sale of AOL shares. The company has also been able virtually to clear itself of debt.

Such prudent financial management is in sharp contrast to the enormous debts and promises of future pots of gold that have been the mark of so many companies in this field. To quote Middelhof again:

> *Despite the recession and the negative repercussions of* 11
> *September, Bertelsmann is able to do business with considerable*
> *capital backing and the clout that accompanies it. We have done a*
> *lot to get to this point: the corporate divisions are drawing together*
> *under the terms of the Bertelsmann Excellence Initiative, new*
> *markets are being opened, and previously unused revenue potential*
> *is being tapped … We have taken advantage of the positive overall*
> *earnings situation to manoeuvre ourselves into a good starting*
> *position for when the economy starts up again. This involved*
> *extensive measures to cut costs, streamline the portfolio, and increase*
> *earnings.*[13]

Over the past three years, Bertelsmann has invested more than €6 billion in the content business, and has strengthened its TV business; 50 per cent of its declared assets are now in television, radio, TV production and sports rights. Regarding sales on the internet, Bertelsmann is the worldwide number one in the music sector and the world's number two in book sales. Internet start-up losses, which peaked at €866 million in 2000–2001, have been reduced to

€226 million. Bertelsmann follows the principle of financing internet start-up losses from capital gains realised on divestments in
other areas.

The Fourth Deadly Sin

Covetousness of the Corporate Joneses

Embrace change – for better or for worse

G urus. The bane of the business world. Always coming up with something new. And the terrible thing is that you simply don't count if you are not a follower of that hitherto-unknown expert, who apparently worked wonders for the nondescript little company that is now causing you so many problems. So – you simply have to follow the trend, don't you? And you have to keep following the trends. Gurus come and gurus go. But change is here to stay. Isn't it?

Sin-O-Meter for Covetousness

We all have our idols, examples that we want to follow. But how often does doing this translate into covetousness? Answer these questions and see whether you are desperately trying to keep up with the Corporate Joneses.

1 You are asked to describe your most important task in the organisation. Do you say: a) creating a new mindset; b) streamlining the organisation; c) implementing a company-wide change process?

2 Your company is facing increasing competition across the board. Do you: a) tell your people that the market is changing and they will have to change too; b) analyse your existing core competencies to see how they can be better leveraged; c) announce a company-wide cost-reduction programme?

3 Your new product bombs. Is your reaction: a) change the design; b) change the advertising; c) change everything you can think of?

4 'The only constant in business is change.' Do you say this: a) occasionally; b) four times a day; c) as many times as you can?

5 You are asked to name your company's most important asset. Do you: a) put on a modest face and look down at your desk; b) talk about the number of patents your company owns; c) say, without hesitation, 'its people'?

6 A rising star applies for a position in your company. Do you: a) tell him what function he will be expected to fulfil and the salary scale linked to that function; b) talk to him about his golf handicap; c) ask him what he will be able to contribute to your operations?

7 You have implemented a company-wide change programme

and are now assessing its success. Do you: a) congratulate your-self on the number of jobs you have eliminated; b) check whether there has been a decline in the number of customer complaints; c) start jotting down catchy names for the next change operation?

8 Take this word-association test. Change: a) attitude; b) always; c) staff cuts.

9 A new company has just entered your market with some inter-esting ideas and a totally fresh approach. Do you: a) change your organisation to match theirs; b) commission a research analyst to discover 'who's behind them'; c) learn from their new manage-ment approach?

10 How many change operations have you experienced during your career? a) 2; b) 12; c) lost count?

Scores

1 a) 1; b) 6; c) 12
2 a) 3; b) 1; c) 4
3 a) 3; b) 3; c) 8
4 a) 2; b) 4; c) 9
5 a) 22; b) 2; c) 0
6 a) 6; b) 13; c) 2
7 a) 8; b) 1; c) 25
8 a) 1; b) 4; c) 15
9 a) 4; b) 7; c) 1
10 a) 2; b) 6; c) you think of a figure.

0 ═══════════════════════════════════════ 80

Where are you on the scale? The farther you are to the right, the more covetous you are.

'Organisations worldwide are confronting more turbulent markets, more demanding shareholders and more discerning customers, and many are restructuring to meet such challenges. Their success in making the changes required depends much on the quality of their leadership – not only at the top of the organisation, but also among all managers responsible for operating results.'[1]

If we understand one thing in business life, it is the importance of change. There is simply no getting away from it. Our markets change. Our business environments change. Our customers demand change. And our products change. And they all change with such rapidity that unless we respond immediately with a far-reaching rethink of the way we do business, we know that very soon we could be out of the game.

There is an urgency about all this. If we don't change, we tell everybody prepared to listen, we might as well stop doing business right now. After all, business today is all about change. It is change that drives success. If we don't change, then we're likely to get rusted in. We can't allow ourselves to continue on the safe path. We have to show courage and move forward. What's more, we don't only have to change now, we have to build in change for the future. We have to adopt a mentality of change. We have to embrace it.

And that's exactly what we've done. Change has become the secret formula; the magic wand to wave at the forces of evil gathering at the corporate gate. Disappointing results? Whisper 'major change drive' at the shareholders meeting and the applause will be deafening. The unexpected failure of a new product? Announce changes in corporate R&D or corporate design, and everyone will be convinced of a radical improvement almost overnight. Oh yes, and if you don't get change happening, then think about changing your job.

Changing environment

The awareness of the need for change arose gradually as we moved from the industrial era into the Knowledge-based Economy. Executives of companies who had enjoyed decades of successful growth were suddenly confronted with new, and largely unexpected, obstacles. Increasing competition – how on earth did the Japanese get this good so unexpectedly? – meant that production processes had to be rationalised, quality had to be improved, distribution had to be more streamlined, and after-sales service had to become 'world class'. Certainly, in the areas of quality, production and service, the changing environment demanded a change in both people and processes. People had to become more 'quality conscious', more 'service-oriented', more 'customer-minded'; processes had to become 'market-driven', quality had to be 'built-in', service had to be more than an 'afterthought'.

It became increasingly obvious that, with far-reaching automation, greater product complexity, shorter life-cycles and a growing demand for individualisation, much about the practices of companies firmly rooted in industrial-economy practices would have to change.

And so change found a permanent place on management agendas.

> *When workmen strive to do better than well,*
> *They do confound their skill in covetousness.*
> — William Shakespeare

It's all about attitude

Almost every manager began preaching that change must become an intrinsic part of the corporate attitude. And indeed, as markets develop overnight, as windows of opportunity open for an all-too-brief moment, so we must have the ability to understand the chances that are being presented. Often these chances will come from unexpected sources or directions, and we must have the ability to be able to look over the walls of our corporate playground and understand the changes new products, new markets and new customers will demand.

What we are really talking about here is not so much the ability to implement far-reaching change, but rather the need for a flexibility in thinking that allows us to look farther than the narrow pigeon-holes in which many companies are happy to live.

And this is where the problem lies. Many managers are convinced that flexibility means change. In order to create the attitude of flexibility, they use the antidote of change. They tell everyone that the new flexibility required for success in business requires a change in mentality and in the way we do business.

We need flexibility – and therefore we are all going to change.

The steps of change

And so managers *embrace* change. They understand that it is absolutely vital to develop a new mindset throughout the company, a mindset that does not hold the past as sacred – 'We've always done things this way in the past and that was good enough then' – but rather is forward-looking, understanding that flexibility is of greater importance in today's market than rigidity.

Having embraced change, managers then decide to *encourage* change. They explain to their employees why change is so vital if the company is to survive. We cannot keep on selling cars in any colour as long as it is black if customers actually want a choice, they say. We no longer have to think about 'the way we always did it', but rather about 'the way we could do it better'. They encourage employees to understand that work is no longer functionally oriented – with narrowly defined responsibilities – but rather process-oriented: every person within the company is a customer of the previous activity and a supplier to the next. Managers encourage customer-orientation – satisfy your customer, whether that customer is internal or external.

But for many of them, encouraging change does not bring the necessary improvements fast enough. Impatience kicks in, and they decide to *initiate* change. Company-wide change programmes are announced. Top managers and business gurus are invited to preach sermons to the congregation. They must be brought to salvation. They must be saved in order to save the company.

Yet this, too, does not have the effect that the manager feels is vital. And so he takes the final step down the path of change: he decides to *implement* change. At last the manager is in control. And inevitably he reaches for instruments with which he feels most comfortable: he changes the company by a whole process of restructuring, re-engineering and downsizing. What started as an attempt to change mentalities has ended up as yet another excuse for company-wide 'rationalisation' – and hundreds, if not thousands, of employees suddenly find themselves without work.

Change for them has not brought the promised land of sustainability; it has thrown them into the abyss created by a short-term demand for improved results.

> *Change begets change. Nothing propagates so fast.*
> — Charles Dickens

Change is the antidote

Is it surprising, then, that the announcement of the umpteenth company-wide change drive initiated in the last few years should be greeted by employees with less than total enthusiasm? People who have lived through one change operation after another – the people who wear the 'I Survived Operation Transformation' T-shirts – have come to understand that change processes are rarely directed at better equipping a company for success in the future.

That may be the stated aim. Certainly, some manager or other will say how important it is to change to make the company more competitive, more profitable, more innovative. There'll be a lot of talk about changing to grasp the future, changing to satisfy cus-tomers, changing to become stronger in the market. There'll be a lot of talk about change requiring re-engineering, right-sizing, function rationalisation. There'll be a lot of talk about refocusing business aims, readjusting strategy, redirecting our energies.

And then, when everything has been said, the deed will be done – and another 4,000 jobs will be cut.

Change is revealed for what it is: an order to change jobs!

No influence

The reality is that the people who suffer most from such change programmes are those who have the least influence on what causes them. For there is another fact that is all too evident to everyone: those who have led the company into a position where change is necessary are the ones least likely to be affected by any change process.

Change, you see, doesn't happen at the top. Change is not something that managers undergo – it is something they implement. When they embrace change, they are really embracing the doctrine of inconsistency. They embrace change as an excuse for doing one thing today and something different tomorrow – 'Circumstances have changed, you see'. They are convinced that a mentality of change means they must implement change at the drop of a hat. In fact, many believe that if they are not implementing change, then in some way they are being negligent. If you're not changing, you're not doing your job. Implementing change has become a substitute for leadership. It is an excuse for strategy. It is an excuse for planning. An excuse for foresightedness. And an antidote for management failure.

Stop change and you stop business.

Stop implementing change and you stop managing business.

Change is one thing, progress is another. 'Change' is scientific, 'progress' is ethical; change is indubitable, whereas progress is a matter of controversy.

– Bertrand Russell

Blunt instrument

And so we reach the heart of the matter: managers use change as a blunt instrument. Change has long ceased to be an attitude of mind, the prerequisite of flexibility; it has become the ultimate synonym for the blunt instrument of downsizing, reorganizing, restructuring, and whatever other 're' is the latest fad. When managers say the company is going to have to change, what they really mean is that, because things have gone wrong in the past, now everybody is going to have to pay the price for previous mistakes. Change is not something that happens to companies; it is something that is inflicted on companies by managers who are trying to get out of a scrape. It is the ultimate blunt instrument in the manager's arsenal.

And it doesn't even work!

Seven out of ten re-engineering projects have failed[2]. Even Stephen Roach, the Wall Street guru whose theories of downsizing resulted in over a million employees being dismissed to save costs admitted in a memo to clients of Morgan Stanley, 'I was wrong.'[3] The author Peter Scott-Morgan agrees: 'Knowing what we know now, to persist in the extreme forms of macho re-engineering … is tantamount to management malpractice. It damages the resilience of the workforce to change.'[4]

All this downsizing has been disastrous to companies everywhere in the world. They reduced their workforce – and threw away the intellectual baby with the industrial bath water. It is impossible to judge how much knowledge has been lost to companies who felt obliged to downsize because everybody else was doing it.

Managers have looked at the successes (so-called) elsewhere

with covetous eyes. They have looked at the Corporate Joneses – and have done everything to keep up with them.

And to make matter worse, they are now realising that the knowledge that has been lost as a result of all these change processes is irreplaceable. They are becoming aware that without the knowledge that they lost when they had to let half of their workforce go, they are finding it almost impossible to compete in today's market place. They need creative vitality – but they've got rid of the people who can provide it.

They now look covetously at the Corporate Joneses who have allowed their businesses to evolve, rather than forcing them to change.

> *Excess of wealth is cause of covetousness.*
>
> – Christopher Marlowe

Change or else …

Many change processes – even those essential if a company is to survive – take place in an atmosphere of threat. People are told that they will have to change – and often are given reasons for this need – but then also told, almost as an afterthought, that if they don't change, they will no longer be welcome in the company.

Is fear the way to create a motivated workforce? Can motivation be improved when employees come to understand that the road to unemployment is paved with the good intentions of change?

And how often *can* people change? This is a crucial question, because what management means by change is: our aims today will not be our aims tomorrow. Our company focus today will not be the same as our company focus tomorrow. And while many employees will understand the need to break with the past, many would also hope that the past is longer than just a few weeks.

Management by change, particularly when it is translated into implementing change, can be totally devastating to a company's morale. And to its performance.

Enforced change creates instability. It creates confusion. It creates the very defensiveness it was supposed to eliminate.

Change is not made without inconvenience, even from worse to better.
— Richard Hooker

Body or soul?

Embracing change means that we acknowledge that the environment in which we are doing business is not static. There is a constant ebb and flow — some may even think of a tidal wave — that sweeps over every single company. Embracing change means developing a new mindset. One that is no longer burdened by the past but prepared to forget it and to be flexible towards the future.

When managers attempt to change attitudes, they come up against a problem: it is difficult — if not impossible — to know for sure whether any change has taken place. How can you ever be certain that people are changing the way they think? How can you ever be certain that employees are once again finely tuned, highly motivated, quality conscious, determined fighting machines? Managers may wish they could get into employees' minds, but they know that ultimately those minds will always remain shut to them. They become frustrated: not only are they unsure that any change has taken place, they can also never be certain that people are now thinking as they would like them to think. There are no dials to show progress; there are no graphs that can track how motivation is improving; there is no test for improved mental flexibility.

Matters of the mind are matters that have to be taken on trust, but trust is the one thing that is often absent in many manager–employee relationships. How on earth can you expect a manager to trust his employees? How can employees be trusted to produce better quality, to listen more carefully to customers, to become more motivated? They have been asked to do so so often in the past – why should they be trusted to do it properly this time? Yet managers have to be able to track improvement. They need figures to show to their management team, their shareholders, their customers, their suppliers. In a world where hard facts are vital, matters of the mind cannot be taken on trust. And thus trying to track changes in motivation, in the soul of the company, will ulti- mately end in failure. It simply cannot be done.

Trust is a two-way street: employees are just as reluctant to trust management. After all, why should an employee trust a manager who announces a change programme aimed at increasing motiva- tion, yet actually implements a drastic resizing operation costing many people their jobs? How can employees trust managers who talk about changing the soul of the company, only to go to work with the surgeon's knife on its body? And why should an employee trust a manager who says that 'this time' change is vital when that same manager said it was vital last year, and the year before that, and the one before that? Why should the process 'this time' make the company stronger? After all, the previous four change processes resulted in a big reduction in jobs, customers and sales, which, the employee is now told, didn't work out well. 'This time, though' things will be different.

Managers and employees have been concentrating on embracing change when they should have been embracing trust.

Change often makes accepted customs into crimes.

– Mason Cooley

The manager who cried 'change'

Yet, to be honest, trust may very well be the last thing possible in many corporate environments. Too many managers have cried 'change' just once too often. They give the latest change process a fancy name – Operation Turnaround, Operation Corporate Salvation, Operation Excite – and expect employees to buy into it, but once again it isn't the soul of the company that is being changed, but its body that is being given all the attention. As many managers who have embraced change have found, when you change a company's body rather than its soul, at least you can see the results.

I resist change even as I call for it.

– Mason Cooley

'Believe what I say, not what I do'

It has become very politically correct to talk about employees as the company's finest, most valuable assets. This recognises the contribution employees make to the success of a company. Recently, a slogan circulated through Royal Philips Electronics read: 'Philips makes products, but people make Philips'. And similar slogans can be found circulating in the corporate corridors of other companies throughout the world. All aim at stressing the importance of people within the company. But what happens when the business requires fewer people to survive? Are employees more valuable at that point than other assets it may own? Or are they just as expendable as buildings, trucks and last year's products?

Change – and the determination to embrace change – has a lot to do with the confusion that now reigns in many employees' minds. Change, they are told, is a matter of the soul – yet ultimately it is the body that is changed. People are the most valuable assets – yet they are the first to leave when the going gets rough.

Managers want their employees to believe what they say, rather than what they do.

They are asking their employees to close their eyes in faith – and then leap off the cliff. And that's not exactly the best way to go about creating a motivated workforce.

Are employees assets?

As business moved from the Industrial Economy into the Knowledge-based Economy, so our perception of many things changed. In the Industrial past, people were hands that were vital to our operations. Just like our machines and factories and warehouses. If we needed more hands, we simply hired them; if we needed fewer, we fired them. People were assets – tangible assets that were just as replaceable as any other tangible asset.

But then things changed. As automation made manual labour

increasingly something of the past, so people were promised a new Utopia, a place where they could do what they did best – think. People were no longer tangible hands; they had become intangible brains.

At least, that was the theory.

Change processes – and the way managers implement rather than embrace change – show that in this area we are still stuck in the Industrial Age. While change processes are supposed to address the mind – treating people as brains – they actually address the body – treating people as hands. In other words, change processes treat people as tangible assets. Like any other tangible asset, such thinking implies, people can as easily be replaced.

This is Industrial Age thinking at its most archaic. And it is quite simply destructive.

What's more, the way managers perceive employees isn't consistent. When a company is doing well, employees are considered intangible assets, making an important contribution to the knowledge base of the company; when things start going less well, employees slip down the scale, and once again become – for management – tangible assets.

But managers, after all, are allowed to change their minds, aren't they?

Let's change our minds

In fact managers never truly change their *own* minds. They never change their addiction to change. And in the Knowledge-based Economy this is dangerous.

Can we really replace brains as easily as hands? And before you shout 'Of course not', reflect on the implications of your reply. Today we no longer think of people as hands, but instead accept that their mental ability is just as important as their physical ones. Change processes can no longer be directed at what people do, but must be directed fully at how they think. This means that, rather than demanding tangible proof that our change operations have worked, we will have to accept intangible trust.

Yet there are even greater implications – for example, for the way in which we deal with employees. Can we really talk about 'Human Resources Management' if we believe that people are vital for their minds? Can we talk about functions, as if people were neatly programmed to fulfil a specific task? As if they were simply drones, each designed for function seven, level four?

But the most fundamental change – and the scariest, at least for Industrial Age throw-backs – is the implication that people will have to be treated as individuals. This is such a fundamental shift in attitude that many managers find it almost impossible to contemplate. They would, of course, never admit that they cannot think of employees as individuals – with their own unique ideas, and personal knowledge – but they will clothe their Industrial-Age-inspired actions in a cloak of Knowledge-based understanding. When they proclaim, 'Let's change our minds', they are still thinking of the ultimate body count. When they acknowledge that people are brains, their thoughts still turn to the headcount.

'Without a detour'

Imagine this: one day a letter arrives from your employer. It tells you about the need for change. Your employer is convinced that unless there is massive change, the whole company could face bankruptcy. You are one of the employees who can no longer be guaranteed a job. You are offered the following choice: you can leave voluntarily and accept a golden handshake based on the number of years you have been employed, or you can decide to wait and see how the cookie crumbles and whether you are one of the fortunate people who keep their jobs or one of the unfortunate ones who are going to lose theirs. Oh, and by the way, the letter informs you, we won't be getting rid of people as much as dispensing with 6,250 functions; you will just have to wait to see whether your function still exists after the reorganisation process has been finalised. In other words, they add, the decision will not take into account the ability or merit of any specific employee; it will not be about people but about function: 6,250 functions will cease to exist – and with them, employment for between 8,000 and 9,000 people.

Body or brain?

This is the letter that was received in September 2001 by some 22,000 Dutch employees of ABN AMRO, Holland's largest Triple A bank. The reorganisation didn't come as a total surprise: most of the bank employees believe that something has to be done to make the bank more competitive and more efficient in the future. At the time it was large and ponderous; it was certainly not the type of lean, flexible organisation that is required for improved profits. But serious doubts have now been raised about the way the company has handled this change process until now.

You would have thought that a bank – particularly one belonging to the top twenty banks of the world – would have been more aware of the Knowledge-based Economy than that. By subjecting their employees to a change process that had all the characteristics of a national lottery, the management – determined to create a bank that offered better prospects for future growth, and better shareholder value – were in danger of ending up with a bank with indifferent service, personnel who lack motivation and drive, and ultimately a second-class organisation with limited sustainability.

The bank had made a decision – one that was negotiated with the trade unions – to treat its employees as bodies. They had agreed to decide which functions would no longer be required in the new, leaner organisation rather than to decide which people would no longer be necessary.

Performance doesn't matter

So what message did this send to the staff? Quite simply that the way they performed was a matter of indifference to the bank. The bank had decided not choose those who stayed on merit. They would not look at experience, knowledge, ability, loyalty or expertise. They would simply look at functions; people who held functions that were no longer required would be asked to leave.

At the time, the bank argued that by concentrating on functions, they were being as fair as possible to the employees. Scraping functions allows management to concentrate on what was really required of the new organisation, rather than being forced to decide between Mr X, who had been with the bank for sixteen years and had two children approaching college age, and Mr Y, who had just joined the company but had been earmarked for a career of some significance within the bank. By choosing functions, management avoided making choices between people.

Funnily enough, the employees didn't see it this way at all. They felt that all the time, energy and effort they had given to the bank had been of no value. They felt that it made no difference to management whether they did their work well or not. Some felt that they could just as well leave things undone; many refused to help an overworked colleague – particularly if that colleague belonged to the 25 per cent whom the bank considered essential for its future.

Brains for sale

The trouble with reducing the headcount is that you also reduce the brain count at the same time. In a highly competitive, knowledge-rich environment, such as international banking, brains and knowledge are of almost inestimable value. The quality of knowledge and brainpower employed by the bank will be of far greater influence to creating a competitive edge than the number of people it employs. Certainly, a reduction in salary costs could result in one of those financial engineering ploys that are used to improve shareholder value; but reducing employees with no regard for the quality of the people retained will not lay the foundations for a sustainable future.

What's more, the people most likely to take advantage of the severance-pay deal – such as offered by ABN AMRO – are those who feel most confident in their ability to find a new employer. In other words, the bank did not only encourage its best people to leave, it had also offered to pay them to leave as well! With this 'Operation No Detour', ABN AMRO placed itself firmly back in the Industrial Age. It treated people as hands, not brains. It placed greater value on the number of people employed than on the experience, knowledge, and motivation of those employees.

It seemed a recipe for creating a third-rate operation at a time when the best is only just good enough.[5]

A change of heart

In the wake of the first wave of negative reactions caused by the letter, ABN AMRO's chairman, Rijkman Groenink, publicly admitted that he regretted handling the matter as he had done. 'The letter caused considerable anger,' he is quoted as saying, 'and I deeply regret that. We did not fully appreciate how hard the message was. Of course, the people who received the letter saying they were "dispensable" were not automatically fired – but that was the idea that was created. People thought they were doomed. All those involved in the negotiations, including the unions, failed to see this in advance. In retrospect, we should have offered everybody the same option. We should not have made the distinction. Perhaps some people would have left that we would have preferred to keep. But we would not have had all these terribly upset and demotivated employees.'[6]

A changing banking environment

Today the business of banking is under enormous pressure. Just a look at one of the recent headlines – 'JP Morgan axes jobs as it seeks 20 per cent cut in costs' [7] – shows just how great that pressure is. The article tells how, in the first two rounds of redundancies, the bank reduced a combined JP Morgan and Chase headcount of 102,000, the largest number of any bank, by 7,000. But, it points out, Dresdner Kleinwort Wasserstein has axed the biggest proportion of its staff, shedding more than 17 per cent of its 8,500 employees in the same year.

Investment banks such as Goldman Sachs, Merrill Lynch, and JP Morgan Chase have all pruned back their main activities. The *Financial Times* comments:

> *Merrill Lynch is to offer a severance deal to all its 65,900 employees on Monday, a move that is likely to result in Wall Street's most sweeping lay-offs as the securities industry contends with a slowing economy and falling profits. Although voluntary severance packages have been common on Wall Street this year, none has been on the scale of the Merrill package. The severance package, which could total more than a year's salary to employees if they agree to resign by early November, is part of an effort by the world's largest brokerage to restructure its far-flung operations. Like other Wall Street firms, its investment-banking revenues have dried up as mergers and acquisitions activity and equity underwriting have gone quiet. Merrill said it had already cut 6,800 employees – 9 per cent of staff – since last year's third quarter. The broker took $152 million in severence costs during the most recent quarter. Still, David Komansky, Merrill's chairman, said on Thursday that the broker was 'sized inappropriately' and that steps would be taken to correct that. All of Merrill's 65,900 employees will be offered voluntary retirement on Monday in*

exchange for what the company calls a 'generous' severance package.[8]

The changes implemented at Holland's largest Triple A bank in 2001 were in line with the general trend throughout the banking industry. Whether the adopted approach – in which quantity is considered before quality – was the right one remains to be seen.

Skandia's successful rejuvenation

Skandia, the Swedish-based insurance company, was founded in 1855. It became something of a national institution, offering employment to generation after generation. But in the 1990s, it decided to transform itself into a business of today. It withdrew from what had traditionally been its core business – property and casualty insurance – and concentrated on marketing life insurance products, notably variable annuities, and offering a broad range of mutual funds. Although that decision meant that staff levels were reduced by about a third, the company today still employs nearly 8,000 people, although now only a third work in Sweden, and 90 per cent of the business is generated outside its home country.

But the area of biggest change has been in the way Skandia deals with its employees. It was one of the first companies to understand the importance of intellectual capital, and even devised a methodology for measuring its value to the company as a whole. Skandia explains this as follows: 'We hire for attitude and train for skills. Or hire the best people and leave them alone.'

In a recent article in *Fortune*, one of the architects of people development at Skandia, Ola Remsted, head of human resources, recalls:

> *in the mid-1990s Skandia was in a financial crisis, battered by hostile takeover attempts. It was then that the company embarked on its drive to 'let people take on responsibility, decide what to do for themselves' rather than be told what to do. We have many new ideas coming from our employees because they feel they have control. The old command-and-control relationship can never be put in again.* [9]

A fanatic is one who can't change his mind and won't change the subject.
– Sir Winston Churchill

Change is essential

It is vital that we embrace change. It is essential if a company is to remain sustainable in the future. But it must be Knowledge-based change, not Industrial-Age change.

It must be change directed at brains, not at bodies.

Managers must come to understand that change frequently happens outside a company. Embracing change means adopting an attitude that allows a fast, flexible and profitable response to that change.

Embracing change does not mean that a company has to be constantly involved in one change programme after another. Sometimes changing is the last thing a company should do. And it is exactly when change becomes a management approach – we will change to this today, to this tomorrow, and to this the day after – that it becomes a sin.

And a sin that must be avoided at all costs.

CASES

The sinner: Ford

Ford Motors is, perhaps more than any other company operating today, a symbol of the Industrial Economy. Yet not long ago the company realised that it was simply impossible to continue operating in the way it did at the start of its life. With growing competition, pressure on prices and higher environmental and consumer standards, car companies do not have things all their own way.

Ford concentrated on reinventing itself. It discovered that there is little money to be earned from the mere sales of automobiles. Building automobiles does not make money; the ancillary services do. Things like financing, insurances, project management, and so on.

And so Ford announced that it was

radically reshaping itself to offer the customer an experience instead of just a finished product. It is separating component-making activities into a distinct company, Visteon, which it may in time spin off. And it is handing over more of the responsibility for manufacturing to subcontractors. At the same time, it is acquiring automotive service companies, such as the Kwik-Fit exhausts-and-brakes chain in Europe, car-recycling businesses in America and the consumer-arm division of Japan's Mazda. It has even signed a deal to provide drivers with satellite-fed audio and other services for a monthly fee. These sit alongside the firm's huge existing consumer-finance business and its Hertz car-rental subsidiary. Whereas automobile makers are lucky to scrape operating margins of more than 5 per cent from actually making cars, other businesses such as leasing, renting and car repair can all achieve margins of 10–15 per cent.[10]

Ford began positioning itself as a 'worldwide supplier of products and services in the field of mobility'. The word 'automobile' was, apparently, no longer used at Ford!

But then ...

Oh dear, it all sounded so promising. Yet now Ford has announced that it is abandoning its plans and 'returning to its core business'. Saint or sinner – you decide.

The saint: Nokia

Let's face it, a company that started in 1865 as a paper manufacturer and is now the world leader in mobile phones – selling more than three times the number of phones than its nearest rival, Motorola – must have changed a little in its 140-year history. And it did: from paper to rubber to cables. And then to the hi-tech world of mobile phones. Yet today it is not so much change that has catapulted Nokia to the Fortune Top 100 list; rather it is its in-built attitude of flexibility that has given it such a remarkable success.

The 'Nokia Way' is its mission statement; it stresses openness, integrity, teamwork, humility and accountability. And the mentality in the company – something that newcomers can find rather daunting – is one of flexibility. A British employee says, 'You join Nokia and no one will give you a very accurate job description. You don't know who your boss is. So you live in this state of confusion – it never goes away. You have to adapt to it.'[11] Other employees explain that job rotation is the rule – some employees say that they have to reprint their business card every two years. And people used to working in a culture that promotes 'getting to the top', may be surprised that Nokia actually promotes something called 'downing the ladder'. Top managers – even vice-presidents – are encouraged to move into different jobs in order to gain experience in new areas of the business.

Similarly, employees are encouraged to work in the most congenial surroundings. The head office of Nokia in Helsinki is a stunning building, but it is what is inside that counts. Employee facilities include a sauna, a cut-price cafeteria, a medical service that provides instant referrals free of charge, and one of the most breathtaking views across the Bay of Finland to downtown Helsinki. But some employees prefer to work out of Scotland or even Los Angeles.

At Nokia, change gurus are a luxury they are quite prepared to live without. Why preach change when it is already so firmly rooted in the mentality of the company? And it is perhaps this environment of flexibility that has allowed Nokia to react so swiftly in a market place where speed is so essential.

The Fifth Deadly Sin

Gluttony for Growth

Own it all – and still want more

et's face it, we live in a Knowledge-based Economy. So it stands to reason that the more knowledge you have, the more successful you can become. As simple as ABC. The trouble is that the moment you've got hold of one piece of knowledge, a new piece comes along. So you have to have that as well. Gluttony can't be a sin when you're talking about owning things. After all, a company never got big (and important) without acquisitions and takeovers. Hell, if you don't do it, somebody else will. More is better – most is best.

Sin-o-Meter for Gluttony

Are you eager to make your company the biggest, the best, the fattest? Do you want to ensure your company's independence by owning as much intellectual property as possible? Then you may be guilty of the sin of gluttony. Answer these questions honestly, and find out just how greedy you are.

1. Your competitor announces that they will be introducing a new operating system in the coming months. Do you: a) tear your hair out, shouting at everyone in the office; b) smile and say, 'It'll never work'; c) tell your lawyers to buy the company?

2. Your IP manager requests an appointment. Do you: a) tell your secretary to deal with it; b) say in surprise, 'I never knew we had one'; c) discuss a strategy with him for generating further income with your IP?

3. Your company owns a lot of patents. Do you: a) keep them safely protected by every means possible; b) license them out to your competitors; c) ask, 'What are patents?'

4. How many acquisitions has your company made during the last three years? a) 3; b) not enough; c) too many?

5. You need to get a new product to market within a very short deadline. Do you: a) tell everyone that they will need to work even longer hours; b) form a joint venture with one of your competitors; c) buy up the competition?

6. You are developing a new product. Do you see it as: a) a way of leveraging your existing knowledge; b) a way of growing the company; c) a way of clobbering the competition?

7. Sustainability means: a) owning all the knowledge for every product; b) creating a world-class R&D department; c) knowing who knows what?

8 You are developing a strategy for knowledge management and invest heavily in it. Do you invest most in: a) the IT department; b) the R&D department; c) the HR department?

9 Give your definition of a world-class company. Is it: a) a company with a proven record of innovation; b) a company that has grown large enough to be self-sufficient and independent; c) a company that owns nothing but can do anything?

10 Did the concept for your latest product arise: a) internally; b) externally; c) from somewhere 'out there'?

Scores

1 a) 3; b) 2; c) 9
2 a) 4; b) 6; c) 0
3 a) 2; b) 1; c) 11
4 a) 3; b) 9; c) 1
5 a) 4; b) 1; c) 15
6 a) 1; b) 3; c) 7
7 a) 6; b) 5; c) 0
8 a) 1; b) 1; c) 1
9 a) 4; b) 8; c) 0
10 a) 1; b) 4; c) 0

0 ═══════════════════════════════════ 80

Where are you on the scale? The farther you are to the right, the nearer you are to bursting your seams!

'Much of today's merger boom is driven by a desperate search for new ideas. So is the fortune now spent on licensing and buying others' intellectual property. According to the Pasadena-based Patent & License Exchange, trading in intangible assets in the United States has risen from $15 billion in 1990 to $100 billion in 1998, with an increasing proportion of the rewards going to small firms and individuals.'[1]

Companies are increasingly coming to understand the importance of knowledge. As the technology content of products increases and new services emerge, so there is a desperate need to own the knowledge that is at the heart of these technologies and services. For owning key knowledge gives a company a strategic advantage over the competition. It makes a company independent, and thus gives it a greater chance of prosperity.

For many companies with roots in the Industrial Economy, all this is business as usual. Traditionally the way to succeed was to control every single aspect of the process chain – from fundamental research to final distribution. It ensured that a company had sufficient internal strength to survive anything the competition was able to concoct. Owning assets – both tangible assets such as plants, processes and buildings, and intangible assets in the form of patents, process knowledge and technological abilities – was seen as the only way for a company to maintain its independence and thus its invulnerability.

Now, of course, knowledge is the currency – and many companies are determined to fill their internal knowledge gaps as quickly as possible. Many go on the acquisition trail

Recently, the European head of Cisco was quoted as saying, 'There has never been a more dramatic time to take market share. We are generating $1.4 billion of free cash every ninety days, so the company has infinite options.' And the report continued, 'Cisco is also back on the acquisition trail. To date, it has made seventy-four acquisitions, eight of which are in Europe. "We probably expect to acquire eight to ten companies over the next year," says Mr Lloyd. "The strategy hasn't changed. We are looking for companies, small and mid-sized, with key technologies ... smaller companies that we can roll into our own sales and marketing and distribution engine and so get huge leverage."' [2]

> *There is a difference between eating and drinking for strength and mere gluttony.*
>
> – Henry David Thoreau

Acquisition lust

In a recent article in *Fortune*, this corporate gluttony was illustrated as follows:

> *WorldCom founder Bernard Ebbers liked to eat. He ate MCI. He ate MFS and its UUNet subsidiary. He tried to eat Sprint. Wall Street helped him wash it all down with cheap capital and a buoyant stock price. Pretty soon, WorldCom was tipping the scales at $39 billion in revenues. But there was a problem: Ebbers didn't know how to digest the things he ate. A born deal-maker, he seemed to care more about snaring new acquisitions than about making the existing ones – all seventy-five of them – work together. At least Ebbers was upfront about it: 'Our goal is not to capture market share or be global,' he told a reporter in 1997. 'Our goal is to be the number one stock on Wall Street.'* [3]

We wonder whether he would have been able to resist that teeny-weeny piece of chocolate offered by waiter John Cleese to the glutton in *The Meaning of Life*!

Innovation still priority

Recently, PricewaterhouseCoopers, one of the world's leading consultancies, published the results of a survey of 150 corporate leaders. Those surveyed underlined that they still valued innovation

> *despite cutbacks and shrinking revenues. The survey of CFOs and managing directors found that 81 per cent of top technology industry executives say innovation has been made an organisation-wide priority in their businesses. And of that group, 54 per cent rate their business's level of innovation as superior to that of their one or two strongest competitors − 17 per cent say 'much better', and 37 per cent say 'somewhat better'. Also, this group expects to grow revenues over the next year 25 per cent faster than their peers who have not embraced innovation. 'Today's continuous, rapid advances in technology make innovation critical not only for individual businesses, but also for our entire economy,' says George Bailey, an innovation expert at PricewaterhouseCoopers. 'Fresh ideas lead to new and better products and services that are worth a premium to customers. Moreover, innovation is freeing workers to do their jobs more efficiently, creating additional value for their employers.' Innovation has had a positive impact for these companies in many areas, with the greatest impact being felt in new product and service development (83 per cent), followed by revenue (80 per cent),*

earnings or profit margins (77 per cent) and efficiency (72 per cent).
The survey was conducted by BSI Global Research Inc. for
PricewaterhouseCoopers' 'Technology Barometer' series.[4]

For many companies, the tradition of in-house research was something of which they could be proud. Many boasted of the many breakthrough inventions, the many patents, the many new technologies that had been created from within the company. It was, many felt, a source of strength, a tradition that gave them a competitive edge.

And as the world moved slowly but surely into the Knowledge-based Economy, many companies were convinced that these established in-house resources would be the key to continued success. After all, if the economy depended on ideas, what company would be better placed for success than one with a tradition of creating such ideas?

Yet few of these companies fully understood how the combining of technologies, the gradual but noticeable blurring of boundaries between areas that until then had been worlds apart, would ultimately leave research-rich companies locked out in the cold.

Many companies discovered, somewhat to their surprise, that what they had thought was the whole picture was little more than a segment. The world had suddenly expanded – and many mighty companies found themselves stranded on a desert island.

But still the desire to do it themselves seemed the primary goal of many companies rooted in the Industrial Economy. Acquisitions – frequently based on the desire to obtain technology that was lacking – became the order of the day. The desire to know it all became essential. And as the world turned digital, so the need for knowledge in a broader range of areas became essential.

For many companies, the painful truth began to dawn: you own all the knowledge in the world, but you are still being beaten to the market by other far less knowledgeable companies. How on earth could that be possible?

We might hypothetically possess ourselves of every technological resource on the North American continent, but as long as our language is inadequate, our vision remains formless, our thinking and feeling are still running in the old cycles, our process may be 'revolutionary' but not transformative.

— Adrienne Rich

Companies don't know what they know

Part of the problem is that few companies fully understand the knowledge that resides within them. Acquisitions may have increased the amount of knowledge, but existing organisational boundaries frequently block the free exchange of that knowledge. And this can be compounded when an acquisition is made on some far-off continent. Or when the culture of the acquiring company does not match that of the acquired company. Instead of owning knowledge, companies suddenly realise that they own only the owners of knowledge! It is almost like having the knowledge neatly filed away in folders on a central computer yet not being able to access a certain folder because you do not have the right password — and, even worse, you have no idea what that folder actually contains.

Knowledge in itself is useless. It is worth nothing. Only when it is put to use can it prove profitable. Only when people have the insight to combine pieces of knowledge in new ways can it provide a breakthrough development. If knowledge is compartmentalised, if management believe ownership is enough and do not stimulate the free flow of knowledge, then all you have achieved is a wealth of data to which no one has access. As the *Economist* describes:

> *Research directors, as well as hi-tech industrialists, now tend to believe that the company-owned research lab, that proud nineteenth-century invention, has become obsolete. This explains why, increasingly, the development and growth of a business is taking place not inside the corporation itself but through partnerships, joint ventures, alliances, minority participation and know-how agreements with institutions in different industries and with a different technology. Something that only fifty years ago would have been unthinkable is becoming common: alliances between institutions of a totally different character, say a profit-making company and a university department, or a city or state government and a business that contracts for a specific service such as cleaning the streets or running prisons.* [5]

Dare to share?

It's all very well to enter into an alliance with a janitorial company – but it's a whole different ball game to expect companies to share knowledge. And if you *have* to share knowledge, then only do it with a supplier – never with a competitor.

Yet that is *exactly* what companies must learn to do if they wish to achieve any sort of sustainability. It is simply not possible to know everything. We would even maintain that it is *undesirable* to want to know everything. Business is not about gathering knowledge, it is about putting knowledge to work. It is about finding new combinations of knowledge that can lead to a win–win situation for the partners concerned.

It was undoubtedly this determination that led to arch-rivals Philips and Sony pooling their knowledge to develop a common standard for the audio CD. Ultimately, both companies benefit from the licensing fees they receive for their joint invention – and these are much more attractive than the high levels of investment and the loss of revenue that could have resulted if the two companies had decided to go head-to-head in a standards war.

And the attractiveness of such alliances will only increase as the ongoing integration of technologies continues. The market will be full of not only competitors, but also potential customers, suppliers and alliance partners. As authors Gary Hamel and C. K. Pralahad point out, 'On any given day, for example, AT&T might find Motorola to be a supplier, a buyer, a competitor *and* a partner.'[6]

Today's digital world demands a range of knowledge that few companies can possibly master alone. As entertainment, information, communication and processing abilities merge, so the range of technologies that even the simplest products require increases. The days of self-contained, heavily barricaded monoliths are gone for ever.

Is it sweet
to possess utterly?
or is it bitter,
bitter as ash?

– Hilda Doolittle

Blinkered

Or are they? Certainly there are enough examples – see Cisco, quoted earlier on p. 116 – of companies that are still determined to own knowledge. Yet one has to wonder whether the ownership of such knowledge will ever lead to major breakthrough products, services or technologies.

Many large companies become blinkered. They may understand the market, the customers, the products and the technologies, but they seldom have the ability to think outside their traditional areas of expertise. Many seem to adopt the policy of acquiring more knowledge in order to do more of the same. They see potential products *within their own environment.* They ignore – or are simply unaware of – potentials that may take them into newer and more profitable territories.

Here is the story of two companies that manufactured doors. Both decided to develop a mission statement. One wrote, 'We will strive to be the leader in quality doors.' A noble aim. The other, however, wrote, 'We will strive to be the leader in entrance technology.' Few companies today have the ability to look beyond traditional boundaries. And owning all the knowledge in the world will not provide them with a wider view of their potential. Most companies remain at best 'leaders in quality doors'; it requires visionaries to become 'leaders in entrance technology'.

Yet this is one of the areas where alliances can prove particularly beneficial. Suddenly a company is confronted with a new culture, a new way of working, a different way of thinking. The exposure to differences can be stimulating – for both parties. And it can lead to a situation in which both parties profit from the alliance. After all, there are so many areas of crossover today that a limited view of one's own industry and market can often prove detrimental. *The Economist* observes:

> *Practically no product or service any longer has either a single specific end-use or application, or its own market. Commercial paper competes with the banks' commercial loans. Cardboard, plastic and aluminium compete with glass for the bottle market. Glass is replacing copper in cables. Steel is competing with wood and plastic in providing the studs around which the American one-family home is constructed.'* [7]

If you are a glass manufacturer, can you possibly understand the bottling, construction and cabling markets? And if you can, will you still be open to new applications and new markets? Is it not better, therefore, to adopt an open-minded policy to enable you to be ready – eager, even – to participate in alliances that could widen your competitive area even further?

> *What one doesn't understand one doesn't possess.*
> – Johann Wolfgang von Goethe

Growing the business

For many managers, the greatest challenge is to grow the business: increased turnover, increased sales, increased staff, increased production facilities, increased office space – all leading, hopefully, to increased profits. There is the underlying conviction that in order to do more, you need more. The more you own, the thinking goes, the more you can do. And the bigger you get, the stronger you become.

That's exactly what Goliath thought!

Today, the true challenge is not to do more with more, but to do more with less. And we're not just talking about the 'lean machine' that became so popular in the 1980s. We are talking about the ability to understand – truly understand – the core competencies of a company and to leverage those competencies without being burdened down by a whole lot of tangible assets.

Difficult? Perhaps. But there are examples of companies who have exploited their core competencies without owning anything.

Why own the buildings?

A number of companies in Europe have discovered that owning assets is not the most lucrative way of earning income from them. Landall Green Parks, Gran Dorado and Euroase were all in the business of owning and operating bungalow parks. They ran the bungalows and the facilities in the parks, renting the accommodation out to visitors in the same way as hotels rent out rooms. But recently, these companies have chosen to make the most of their core competency, managing the parks, and sold off all the bungalows to private investors. They now concentrate fully on renting out the accommodation on behalf of the owners, taking a healthy 25 per cent fee for their activities. The maintenance of the bungalows is now the responsibility of the investors – who have also accepted the risk of non-occupancy – and any costs involved in upkeep are invoiced through to them.

These companies have found a very profitable way of commer-

cialising their knowledge and creating profits from a core competency that does not require the ownership of anything.[8]

> *Knowledge is not eating, and we cannot expect to devour and possess what*
> *we mean. Knowledge is recognition of something absent;*
> *it is a salutation, not an embrace.*
>
> – George Santayana

Enjoy the benefits

Progressive companies today are discovering that a real competitive
advantage can be gained not by owning assets – whether intangible
or tangible – but rather by enjoying the benefits of those assets.

The pharmaceutical industry is at the cutting edge of innovation. It is constantly searching for new products that can combat
disease – and rake in billions of dollars in revenue. Yet while the
industry spends astronomical amounts on research, it does not shut
its doors to research done elsewhere. In fact, early-stage research is
conducted entirely by entrepreneurs in small companies which
then sell it on to the big firms when they reach expensive, risky
clinical trials. According to *The Economist,* 'around a third of drug
firms' total revenue now comes from licensed-in technology.' [9]
And, recently, Genfit announced strategic alliances aimed specifically at research. *La Tribune* reported:

> *Lille-based biotech Genfit has signed two strategic agreements with*
> *BioMerieux-Pierre Fabre (BMPF) and Laboratoires Fournier worth*
> *a total of €10 million. The three-year alliance with BMPF will*
> *involve joint research into the identification of the patterns of*

*molecular action created by new drugs which could in future be used
to treat cardiovascular problems. Meanwhile, under the terms of its
five-year partnership with Fournier, Genfit will look into new
treatments for metabolic illnesses.* [10]

Even in the automobile industry – still considered by many the bastion of industrial thinking – such alliances are becoming increasingly frequent. *The Economist* again:

*Eighty years ago, GM first developed both the organisational
concepts and the organisational structure on which today's large
corporations everywhere are based. It also invented the idea of a
distinct top management. Now it is experimenting with a range of
new organisational models. It has been changing itself from a
unitary corporation held together by control through ownership into
a group held together by management control, with GM often
holding only a minority stake. GM now controls but does not own
Fiat, itself one of the oldest and largest car-makers. It also controls
Saab in Sweden and two smaller Japanese car-makers, Suzuki and
Isuzu. At the same time GM has divested itself of much of its
manufacturing by spinning off into a separate company, called
Delphi, the making of parts and accessories that together account for
60–70 per cent of the cost of producing a car. Instead of owning – or
at least controlling – the suppliers of parts and accessories, GM will
in future buy them at auction and on the internet. It has joined up
with its American competitors, Ford and DaimlerChrysler, to create
an independent purchasing co-operative that will buy for its
members from whatever source offers the best deal. All the other car-
makers have been invited to join. GM will still design its cars, it
will still make engines and it will still assemble. It will also still sell*

its cars through its dealer network. But in addition to selling its own cars, GM intends to become a car merchant and a buyer for the ultimate consumer, finding the right car for the buyer no matter who makes it. [11]

Another example is the research programme developed by Alcatel, a company that builds next-generation networks, delivering integrated end-to-end voice and data communication solutions to established and new carriers, as well as enterprises and consumers worldwide. With 120,000 employees and sales of €21.3 billion, Alcatel operates in more than 130 countries.

In a recent press release, the company announced a 'unique' programme, the aim of which was to 'reinforce innovation efforts and to sharpen its competitive edge by promoting closer long-term relationships with key universities and research institutes around the world. The programme will apply to all areas of research and innovation of interest to Alcatel.' [12]

The Alcatel Research Partner Program combines three types of collaboration in a worldwide scheme which the press release summarises as follows:

Research collaboration: Alcatel will provide select research partners with unique opportunities to collaborate with Alcatel's research community. Alcatel and the research partner will participate in scientific and technological development activities together to the benefit of both partners.

Mobility, training and education: Alcatel and the research partner will support and facilitate the exchange of researchers and students, through temporary assignments of researchers and professors, fellowships and offers of employment for students.

Early-stage companies programmes: The partnership is open to early-stage companies programmes within the university or institute to commercially leverage innovative ideas.

Alcatel's chief technology officer, Martin De Prycker, comments: 'The Alcatel Research Partner Program will create opportunities for true collaboration between academia and industry that will cut across geographic and sectorial barriers and should open up exciting new telecommunications research prospects. This confirms Alcatel's commitment to long term research programs.'[13] To date, seven research partners have committed themselves to participate in the programme.

Burdened down

These examples all demonstrate an understanding that a 'go-it-alone' mentality has little place in the Knowledge-based Economy. Owning assets only makes a company fatter; it can never make it more agile.

And, to be quite honest, agility is one of the most important qualities a company can have. For as business moves forward with the speed of fright, so the windows of opportunities become smaller and smaller. There is simply no time for companies to learn everything from scratch. The larger a company becomes, the more knowledge it gathers, the more it feels the need to make use of its own knowledge. For that knowledge implies such an enormous investment that it would be criminal not to put it to use.

The saying goes that a little knowledge is a dangerous thing. We would maintain that too much knowledge is much more dangerous. It causes an inward-looking focus – we must use our knowledge – when an outward focus is required. The more knowledge a company acquires, the more attention it must give to putting that knowledge to some use or other and the less attention it can give to defining answers to customers' – and customers' customers' – needs.

What's more, a company that has acquired knowledge owners may soon find that they have all too quickly outlived their usefulness. Knowledge is not eternal; it does not automatically continue to be useful. A company may have the knowledge to build radio tubes, but it is doubtful whether this knowledge could provide a major breakthrough in today's world.

> *A man can only attain knowledge with the help of those who possess it.*
> *This must be understood from the very beginning.*
> *One must learn from him who knows.*
>
> – George Gurdjieff

Adding value

Many companies have been confused by all the talk about the Knowledge-based Economy. They have set out on a path of gathering knowledge, acquiring knowledge-rich companies, accumulating expertise. And because of this focus, they have lost sight of their true task: to add value.

Owning knowledge is no guarantee of success. That is much more likely to come to those companies that have the agility to *access* the knowledge they need to provide solutions to newly emerging customer needs and demands. These will change –

almost overnight. The speed of change requires a speed of reaction that is only possible to companies not weighed down by assets, whether tangible or intangible.

When opportunities present themselves, it is necessary to leverage the knowledge required quickly and efficiently. Fat, inefficient companies will go out and buy it; agile, responsive companies will go out and use it.

And so we consider the desire to own assets a deadly sin. The path to salvation is to adopt a mentality of benefiting from assets, whether you own them or not.

CASES

The sinner: KirchGruppe

It is a simple philosophy: own it all. The more you own, the more you own. But it is a philosophy that has spelt doom for the German KirchGruppe. The company's complex network of ambitious deals has begun to fray and fall apart, and the house that Mr Kirch built has imploded. KirchGruppe paid its way by creating a staggeringly convoluted network of deals, loans and subsidiaries. And the tapestry was so complex that even with protection from creditors, the many banks and other stakeholders trying to stitch together some means of rescue had a tough task ahead of them.

KirchGruppe, founded in 1954, had long been a succesful media giant. Its founder, Leo Kirch, built a German empire with extensive interests in Switzerland, Spain and Italy, encompassing digital television, software development and the largest international film and TV series licensing firm outside the United States. Together with its arch-rival, media group Bertelsmann, it accounted for 90 per cent of German TV advertising revenue, and competitors feared their financial might and overwhelming advantage in the purchase of sports and film rights. Kirch's purchase, in 1996, of the TV rights for the 2002 and 2006 football World Cup finals for €1.9 billion provided evidence of that power. In 2001, it won a long battle over the television rights for Formula One motor racing for €1.5 billion, leaving the company saddled with about €4.4 billion in debt.

While this empire-building exercise left the company carrying huge debts, its revenues from its key pay-TV services continued to disappoint, despite a restructuring exercise in 1999. Although it had exclusive rights to cover premiership football events, its key pay-TV services had attracted few subscribers – 2.4 million out of about 34 million television households in 2001. The company, hit hard by the global slump in advertising sales, was forced to negotiate an extension of some of its loans with creditor banks in 2001. And its rivals, scenting blood, used their joint ownership of various Kirch assets to claim their optional right of a sale back of these assets to the KirchGruppe to pile on the pressure. The company became undermined by debts, said to total at least €6.5 billion. Kirch had driven more than €3 billion into its pay-TV arm for just 2.4 million subscribers; it was losing €2.3 million a day. The group put its Formula One and World Cup rights up for sale in 2002, cut up to 30 per cent of its workforce as part of a restructuring plan and put its prime money-making asset, Germany's biggest commercial broadcaster, ProSieben, up for sale. The main unit of the Kirch media empire declared itself insolvent in April 2002, in Germany's biggest corporate collapse since the Second World War. Its key pay-TV services went bust in May 2002 and the Kirch holding company was forced into insolvency shortly afterwards. Germany's prestigious Bundesliga, one of the top football leagues in the world, is dependent on the billions of euros KirchGruppe has promised it for TV rights and is trying to deal with the prospect that failed media giant Kirch is highly unlikely to be able to make the promised €200 million in payments for football rights.

The saint: the chip industry

The chip industry doing something right? Surely, it is the one area that has grown large through one simple idea: get to the market first and rake in the big bucks before the competition wakes up. But the dramatic fall in chip demand during 2001 – at 32 per cent, the biggest decline in the history of the industry – began to make the weaknesses of the industry much more apparent. Price erosion, falling demand, a high level of stock-piled inventory, the enormous costs of capital investments and a cut-throat mentality aimed at beating the competition no matter what – all these have resulted in something most commentators would have thought impossible: alliances between competitors.

BBC News reports:

In the latest of a series of cost-sharing alliances in the semiconductor industry, France's STMicroelectronics, the Dutch firm Philips and US Motorola have agreed a $1.4 billion joint venture to develop new-generation chip technology. The three firms plan to enlist Taiwan Semiconductor (TSMC), one of the world's biggest chip firms, as a partner. The announcement represents the expansion of a previous agreement to develop CMOS process chip technology at *a 300mm wafer plant in the French Alpine town of Crolles. Such deals, where once-bitter rivals pool R&D expenses, have become increasingly common in the chip industry, which has been struggling with its worst slump in a decade.*[14]

The Sixth Deadly Sin

Envy in the Workplace

Guarantee quality – and let the figures prove you right

Nothing can be more galling than competitors announcing that they have achieved a quality level of 1 per billion (or trillion, if they're really good). Makes your company look a bit of a fool. Not to mention careless. Or even lackadaisical. So quality drives are the order of the day, as they have been the order of every day for the last four decades. The higher the quality, the better the product, the more satisfied the customer. And, let's face it, higher quality means you can do away with customer service. If something never goes wrong, there's no need to fix it. Nor to listen to all those complains from nit-picking individuals ...

Sin-O-Meter for Envy

You have always wanted your company to be recognised as world-class. And you want to have the figures to prove it. Answer the following questions honestly, and see whether you may be committing the sin of envy.

1 What figures do you use to judge your quality levels? Those reflecting: a) industry standards; b) ISO standards; c) customer feedback?

2 Which of the following statements most accurately reflects your opinion? Is it: a) quality is in the mind of the beholder; b) quality can never be too high; c) quality levels are set by customers?

3 You initiate a company-wide quality drive. Do you direct this primarily at: a) production; b) management; c) research and development?

4 Should quality be: a) designed in; b) tested out; c) taken for granted?

5 Your company has been awarded an ISO certification. Do you: a) throw a party for the whole company; b) send out a press release; c) shrug and continue as you have always done?

6 You are asked to address a meeting of quality specialists. Do you: a) talk about standards; b) talk about people; c) tell them a series of hair-raising stories about the consequences of poor quality?

7 You are asked to choose the most important aspect of your company's quality policy. Do you choose: a) quality of processes; b) quality of environment; c) quality of customer services?

8 A member of the technology group suggests a new quality drive. Do you: a) support him through thick and thin; b) ask him to

catalogue his aims; c) tell him to get on with it?

9 Your company has a reputation for high quality. Do you: a) think this gives you a competitive advantage; b) accept it as a norm for business today; c) state that things can always be improved?

10 You address your management team. Do you tell them to: a) embrace quality; b) create quality; c) forget quality and think about agility?

Scores

1 a) 3; b) 3; c) 1
2 a) 5; b) 6; c) 2
3 a) 7; b) 1; c) 2
4 a) 2; b) 5; c) 0
5 a) 9; b) 15; c) 2
6 a) 4; b) 1; c) 12
7 a) 4; b) 1; c) 1
8 a) 4; b) 1; c) 9
9 a) 4; b) 1; c) 7
10 a) 12; b) 12; c) 1

0 ═══════════════════════════════════ 80

Where are you on the scale? The farther you are to the right, the more envious you are.

'Manufacturers over the last twenty years have invested billions of dollars in various quality-improvement efforts. Among the most popular today are the principles of lean manufacturing as pioneered by Toyota Motor Corp. and the Six Sigma standards that help companies refine their quality efforts to achieve still greater improvements. In most cases, investments in these programmes have been more than recovered by lower production costs, less scrap, fewer defects and reduced warranty expense.'[1]

Quality is one area in which management has succeeded. Perhaps because most quality programmes concentrate on improving the industrial aspects of the business. These are areas in which most managers feel most at home. They can quantify and evaluate and benchmark and re-engineer to their hearts' content. And they can produce figures that show they are getting somewhere.

Nothing appeals to a manager more than demonstrable results. So, all's well in quality land? Well – no.

Industry Week comments:

Most companies haven't got a clue as to what that cost is. 'I've never walked into a plant where anybody knew the cost of quality,' says Kevin Smith, president of Productivity Group, Div. Productivity Inc., Portland, Oregon. 'It's amazing what design engineers don't know about manufacturing,' says Jane Algee, productibility manager for the Comanche helicopter electro-optical sensor system program at Lockheed Martin Missiles and Fire Control in Orlando. Currently on leave of absence in Tokyo, Algee, immediate past president of the Institute of Industrial Engineers, agrees that most product designers have little or no idea of the impact poor design can have on both quality and cost. 'It's eye-opening that a lot of these designers have been in industry over thirty years, yet they don't understand the cost of quality — how pinching a penny now can cost you a hundred times over in the future,' she says. 'It's kind of the American mistake.'[2]

In other words, although companies have invested billions in quality improvement and achieved noticeable results, people are apparently still unaware of how to create quality from the word go.

Managers are often, it seems, envious of success. And allow their envy to get the upper hand.

> *Envy awakens at the sound of a distant laugh.*
>
> — Mason Cooley

Playing catch-up

In retrospect, companies had little choice about quality improvement. It was, like greatness, thrust upon them. As Japanese companies began making inroads into markets that many companies had considered inviolate, so the need for action became urgent.

And that urgency gave rise to the thousands of quality drives that took place in the 1970s and 1980s. It was a matter of catching up — or dropping out of the race altogether. And there were quite a few in the latter category that simply never made the grade. Their indifference to quality relegated them to the category of 'whatever happened to …'

But there was also something else. Many companies were firmly convinced that quality made them competitive. There was a feeling that Japanese companies had won the world with quality – and all western companies had to do to gain back their markets was to match the quality of their competitors. But many soon discovered that playing catch-up was something that they would have to do for a very long time. As soon as they matched the quality of their competitors, they discovered that they had once again raised the bar and set new, even higher standards. They learned – not easily in many cases – that there was no end to quality improvement; it would be an ongoing task as long as business continued.

Yet there was still the notion that guaranteeing quality would automatically guarantee competitiveness. In their book *Competing for the Future*, Hamel and Prahalad discuss a survey held among leading American managers:

> *Nearly 80 per cent of managers polled believed that quality would be a fundamental source of competitive advantage in the year 2000. Yet barely half of Japanese managers predicted quality to be a source of advantage in the year 2000, though 82 per cent believed it was currently an important advantage. Rated first as a source of competitive advantage in the year 2000 by Japanese managers was a capacity to create fundamentally new products and businesses. Does this mean that Japanese managers are going to turn their backs on quality? Of course not. It merely indicates that by the year 2000 quality will no longer be a competitive differentiator; it will simply be the price of market entry. These Japanese managers realise that tomorrow's competitive advantages must necessarily be different from today's.*[3]

Quality provided a competitive advantage then; what about *now*?

The wicked envy and hate; it is their way of admiring.

– Victor Hugo

Base Envy withers at another's joy,
And hates that excellence it cannot reach.

– James Thomson

Are you still thinking about breathing?

By now – in the twenty-first century – quality should have become normal; it should have become so imbedded in a company's culture that it never demands the focus of management. Yet today quality is still high on the agenda of many companies. And by placing it there, managers admit to two failings: first, they have created quality in processes, but have failed to create a culture of quality; second, they have no idea what competitiveness means in today's Knowledge-based Economy.

If you're still thinking about quality, you are doing little more than thinking about breathing. And others are already thinking about running a marathon.

Like so many of the sins we discuss in this book, concentrating on quality betrays management's addiction to the past. It is an area they know. It is an area where they can book results – and prove it with figures. It is still of relevance in industrial operations – the car industry, for example – but in more knowledge-intensive areas, it has little to contribute. How do you judge, for example, the quality of customer service? With little forms at the checkout desks of hotels? Is the inability to generate sales with a new product due to its bad quality – or to its not having a market fit? Was it too late to market? Was the price-setting wrong? Were customers really interested in it in the first place?

Now many people will argue that all these are aspects of quality. And they are right. Or at least they would be right if managers discussed all aspects of business under the heading 'quality'. But we all know that is not the case. Quality still lives in a business vacuum. It means product quality, process quality, administrative quality and even, by extension, organisational quality. It does not mean the quality of competitiveness.

And this is what makes it a sin.

Focusing on quality means that managers are concentrating on the tangible aspects of the business process, rather than on the intangibles.

We have to have somebody to worship and envy, or we cannot be content.

– Mark Twain

Quality bouquets

Recently, we were told the story of an interior plant company that, as supplier to a large multinational, had been required to obtain ISO certification. It was understandably proud of its new certification – it was, after all, the only florist in the city that could prove its quality. One week, one of the employees was asked to work on his day off. There was a shortage of staff that day, he was told, and they needed him to deliver the flowers ordered by customers. He asked whether anybody was ill. No, he was told, the person normally responsible for delivering the flowers had to fill in the ISO forms on that day, so he would not be available.

A quality-certificated company that was unable to deliver its flowers because they had to fill in forms required by the quality certificate? Obtaining ISO certification had not helped the company improve customer satisfaction (customers, after all, are generally satisfied if the flowers they order are fresh and delivered on time); it had, however, helped standardise the administration and invoicing system.

Big deal, we thought in unison.

ISO and ITO are today's Seals of Quality. Yet the very essence of these standards is standardisation. They are concerned with the procedures laid down by some Higher Institute and how closely a company follows them. ISO and ITO provide the rosaries for today's religion of standardisation. Although we by no means reject quality-conscious activities, we do question the need for standardisation. Does a 46-employee florist company need the same sort of procedures as a 250,000-employee multinational? Logic would say no; quality certification institutes argue yes.

Quality programmes are still all too often entirely internally focused. As if quality were made within a company's four walls and then shipped out into the wide world to be admired by all. Yet today, quality is made in the market place. It is there that we find the people that are the most critical of quality.

Of course, many companies have recognised the importance of customer input for a whole range of their activities. And there are a growing number of managers who eagerly embrace customer-relation management systems. Many believe that these hold the key to ultimate quality: customer satisfaction.

But do they? Certainly, they give feedback on a customer's behaviour — however, they can never truly judge whether a customer is truly satisfied or not. And the problem is that customer satisfaction is still a long way below an acceptable level.

Often the irritation is caused by little things. Just recently, one of us purchased a new mobile telephone during a business trip to the Ukraine. It was a reliable brand, well recognised for its quality. But the instructions for use were – in Italian!

Call if you dare!

Yet this irritation is a minor one compared to the frustration felt today by many consumers trying to contact a call centre. Call centres have been heralded as the ultimate means of creating consumer satisfaction. Online day and night, they are there to answer any question a consumer may have regarding a specific product.

Great – until you need to use one. First, you may find it quite a challenge to get in touch with the centre required. And when you do, you may be kept on hold for what often seems like hours on end. When, finally, you are connected to the 'specialist', you may realise that he or she is doing little more than quoting to you from the instruction manual that you have already tried reading, in a vain attempt to solve your problem. Any initiative to go 'outside the book' is carefully squashed. You receive a standard answer – even if your question is far from standard.

Instead of creating customer satisfaction, many call centres actually aggravate the situation. And what's more, the customer has to pay for this aggravation. Call centres ultimately treat customers – the most valued possession of any company – as numbers, as problems that companies would rather not worry about. They have become the hi-tech excuse for quality avoidance.

No wonder that customers are getting tired of this cavalier approach to their problems!

One shining quality lends a lustre to another, or hides some glaring defect.
— William Hazlitt

What about people?

All too often, as we have mentioned, quality thinking as adopted by managers concentrates on processes. On the tangibles. Rarely, if ever, does it deal with people. Yet in today's Knowledge-based Economy, people are the business. The only so-called knowledge that resides in companies is technological data. The ability to conceive new ideas, to make unique connections between existing technologies, to envisage breakthrough technologies, can never be kept on a hard disk. Computers still do not have the ability to think; that they must leave to their creators.

Many would argue that people are given a predominant role in quality-improvement programmes. Many managers will claim that they constantly emphasise that people are a company's most valuable asset. They will argue that they constantly stress the fact that people make quality. What they really mean is: people operate the machines that make quality. And when they talk of people as assets, they imply that, like other assets within a company, they are replaceable. They see people as part of the process – and the one part of the process that they cannot fully control to their satisfaction.

Business today is no longer concentrated in the industrial sector. Increasingly, there is a move towards the service sector. And this relies, more heavily than ever, on people.

145

In any retail and catering operation, success ultimately depends on customer satisfaction. Repeat customers are at the core of the business. Obviously, consistent quality and value for money play an important role, but service is equally vital. Yet in many such operations, the people who give the service – and therefore help create customer satisfaction – are often those who are expected to work for low salaries and poor secondary benefits. The result? In this area, staff turnover is exceptionally high – between 150 and 400 per cent annually. And even the turnover of store managers is traditionally somewhere around 50 per cent per year.

To quote Starbucks' chairman Howard Schultz: 'These people are not only the heart and soul but also the public face of the company. Every dollar earned passes through their hands. If the fate of your business is in the hands of a twenty-year-old part-time worker who goes to college or pursues acting on the side, can you afford to treat him or her as expendable?' [4]

Yet managers who concentrate on process and procedural quality are guilty of doing just that: they treat people as expendable.

To understand the true quality of people, you must look into their minds, and examine their pursuits and aversions.

– Marcus Aurelius

Creating competitiveness

There is, however, a change in the way some companies think about people. And this has resulted in Great Britain in a nationwide scheme, called the Investors in People Standard. This is how they describe themselves:

Investors in People is a national quality standard which sets a level of good practice for improving an organisation's performance through its people. Since 1991, tens of thousands of UK employers, employing millions of people, have become involved with the Standard and know the benefits of being an 'Investor in People'. More than 24,000 organisations are currently recognised as Investors in People and over 24 per cent of the UK workforce are now working with the Standard. The Standard provides a national framework for improving business performance and competitiveness, through a planned approach to setting and communicating business objectives and developing people to meet these objectives. The result is that what people can do and are motivated to do matches what the organisation needs them to do. The process is cyclical and should engender a culture of continuous improvement.

One of the benefits mentioned, 'Enhanced quality investing in people significantly improves the results of quality programmes', deserves being singled out, for it underlines how people and quality programmes have all too often become separated in many managers' minds. Yet unless considerable attention is given to improving the quality of people, the future of a company – even if it achieves zero defects – will look gloomy.

Quality does not provide competitiveness, but quality people can. Tangible assets – the ones constantly under improvement in most quality programmes – matter less; brains matter more.

Managers who wish to guarantee quality must, in today's world, guarantee not quality of processes, but quality of environment. They must understand that today's knowledge professionals – the brains on which success depends – are unlikely to accept employment in an environment that considers them as dispensable as the hands of industrial shift-workers. This new breed of knowledge professionals understands that the knowledge they have acquired and the ability they have to put that knowledge to work can provide a company with enormous benefits. And they expect to be respected. They expect to be part of a challenging environment in which there is an express understanding that success is created not by quality processes but by quality people.

Theo Classen, chief technology officer of Philips Semiconductors, maintains that technology suppliers are no longer judged just on the quality and reliability of their products, but also on the speed with which those products can be developed and brought to market.[5] Speed is something that requires agility of mind and action. It cannot be built into any production process. It is something unique to people. The ability to recognise opportunities, and take steps to leverage the knowledge base of a company to take advantages of those opportunities, is something that is still dependent on people.

Improve the processes if you will; but forget people at your peril.

All things will be produced in superior quantity and quality, and with greater ease, when each man works at a single occupation, in accordance with his natural gifts, and at the right moment, without meddling with anything else.

– Plato

CASES

The sinner: Rolls-Royce

A sinner? Rolls-Royce? Has any company ever achieved the reputation – worldwide – for quality that has set Rolls-Royce apart
from all other car companies?

Certainly, Rolls-Royce has come to be synonymous with top
quality. Its name has been used by companies throughout the
world wishing to claim an undisputed leadership in whatever sector
they happen to compete. The Rolls-Royce of audio equipment;
the Rolls-Royce of the suntan lotions; the Rolls-Royce, even, of
waste-paper baskets.

For many people, Rolls-Royce is the very epitome of the high-
quality, hand-made, luxury, expensive car. Yet today, the car division
no longer belongs to the Rolls-Royce Group. Instead, the group
itself prefers to concentrate on more profitable areas of business such
as turbine engines. Go to the official website of Rolls-Royce and you
will find a simple statement: 'Rolls-Royce Motor Cars Limited is part
of Volkswagen AG and is not a member of the Rolls-Royce plc group
of companies.'

Rolls-Royce as a car company has not been part of the Rolls-
Royce Group since 1971, when it was spun off as an independent
company. Its profits and success declined until, in 1978, it was
acquired by Vickers. Although the motor company gradually
managed improved profitability, in 1998 Vickers decided to sell it.
Vickers chairman, Sir Colin Chandler, said at the time, 'We
believe this is now in the best interests of both Vickers' shareholders and the Rolls-Royce Motor Car business. We have taken
this great business from the low days of the last recession through

to the present high level of investment, to a stage where we are confident its value to Vickers' shareholders has been maximised.' In other words, we will sell now because we are not sure about its future.

A fierce battle broke out for Rolls-Royce Motor Cars between BMW – the logical choice since it had supplied Rolls-Royce with its engines for many years – and Volkswagen. In the end, Volkswagen acquired the company, but BMW, in a private deal with Rolls-Royce plc, acquired the name.

Because by now that was what it was all about. Not the company. Not the motor car. But the reputation. The quality image. And for that – and only that – BMW was prepared to pay $70 million. And the factory? It continues to produce cars. Luxury cars. But from the end of 2002, they will be Bentleys. Without the investments made in the company by Vickers and Volkswagen, Rolls-Royce as a car brand would have long since ceased to exist.

The saint: Porsche

Porsche, the smallest of Germany's six major car-makers is, with a pre-tax net return on sales of 11.9 per cent, the world's most profitable one. Porsche reported a rise in sales and profit at a time when many of the world's leading car-makers were reporting steep falls in profit and, in some cases, big losses.

Mr Wiedeking, Porsche's chief executive, attributed the firm's resilience this time to good engineering, management and distribution. And good-quality engineering is indeed a key feature for Porsche. As a matter of fact, quality has become a key part of the value-added Porsche driving experience for its customers, and offers Porsche a serious competitive edge.

As the company's website says: 'Quality is a point of view. For some it is in the durability of the materials, for others in the fascination of driving. "Porsche quality" means having your cake and eating it.' That some 70 per cent of all Porsches ever built are still being driven clearly demonstrates the exhilaration of the Porsche experience. This company sees meeting this goal in the future not just as another piece of work to be done, but rather as a challenge they have set themselves.

At Porsche, quality must recognise no limits, but what has been achieved can only be the new starting point for future excellence. For example, a Porsche cabriolet's roof will be opened and closed a total of 6,000 times under extremely hot, normal and cold (−10°C) conditions; windows will be rolled up and down 4,000 times; doors will be closed 100,000 times. The testing methods are the result of years of experience. They are, for Porsche, the definition of quality assurance.

'Combine the possible with the seemingly impossible. This is how we still wish to differentiate ourselves from our competitors. And that is intentional. For Porsche, the ultimate test is to exhaust all possibilities for excellence even at the cutting edge of technology. We regard every idea as an opportunity.'

Porsche can only survive as an independent manufacturer in the long term if every procedure and process has been optimised and if still more ways of improving can be found. Both procedure and process are checked every day to see if new ideas can be applied. For Porsche, the goal isn't so much to protect achievements for their own sake, but to use them as potential for the future.

This is true especially of the company's interaction with

customers, and the recent years have shown that Porsche and all its staff have understood this. Take the assembly line in Stuttgart, which cranks out some 145 cars a day. This is no grim industrial setting where workers are all but tethered to their machines. For starters, each car on the line is different. A $40,000 Boxster convertible may precede a $150,000-plus GT2 Carrera with a V-10 engine capable of speeds of more than 200 mph, followed by any one of Porsche's eight other basic models. Each car is customised. Customers have more than a billion possible combinations, when you consider all the options for interiors, seats, dashboards, engine types, body styles, etc. That's in addition to colour. Porsche will paint the car any colour the customer desires, such as the red shade one Texan wanted to match his wife's favourite lipstick. The worker who paints the last three layers scratches his or her name into a space behind the right tail-light. This pleasure in personal responsibility for the work they do is eventually experienced by the customer – experienced in the fullest sense of the word. The belief that less can sometimes be more has guided Porsche on all levels and in all its activities. Productivity at Porsche is a never-ending process of improvement and refinement. Even in the earliest stages of development its production experts and external suppliers sit down together to exchange information and expertise. Porsche has been able to reduce the number of parts it manufactures itself to just 20 per cent. A programme developed by Porsche additionally reduces stocks and guarantees sensible production planning to use all hi-tech resources to the maximum. Stocks and production times were halved from the levels before the restructuring.

Alongside the desired profitability, Porsche achieved a degree of flexibility it had never known before. Every conceivable mix of 911 and Boxster models can now be manufactured on the production line. This really pays dividends when a new series of products is introduced – a production line for profit. In fact, Porsche is now advising other companies on the successful secrets of slimline business through its Porsche consultancy business.

The Seventh Deadly Sin

Pride at the Top

Fix it – no matter what others think

You didn't get where you are by dodging the issues. By opting out of decisions. You do what has to be done, for the good of all. Isn't that why they hired you in the first place? Because of your proven track record? Because you have built up a reputation for getting things done? Important decisions can't be delegated to committees – they require instant attention. From you. Because only you know all the details. Only you are in a position to see the full picture. To know where the company is going. The others simply can't cut it. The others, after all, aren't you …

Sin-O-Meter for Pride

You are known for your fast decision-making, your forthright opinions, your trouble-shooting qualities. You are the one they look to for solutions. But how often are those solutions based on pride? Take the test – and find out how often you are guilty of the sin of pride.

1 Your CFO tells you that your company's profits are under pressure. Do you: a) sell your shares; b) announce a downsizing programme; c) look for new areas where you can improve your performance?
2 You initiate a plan to create a website for your company. Is your main reason: a) to appear progressive; b) to supply surfers with information; c) to generate business?
3 You ask a committee to prepare a recommendation for new business. Do you ask for: a) a detailed analysis of potential profits; b) a summary on one A4; c) just give me what I need to know?
4 You are asked to name your best management quality. Is it: a) the ability to listen; b) quick decisions; c) pushing things through?
5 A report you commissioned suggests a repositioning of your brand. Do you: a) file the report away for later use; b) sack the company you hired to produce it because 'they have no idea about the business we're in'; c) ask for a cost analysis of the plan?
6 You are looking for ways to expand your business. Do you: a) announce a price cut for your existing products; b) acquire a new company that operates in a related but different area; c)

analyse your core competencies to see how they can be better exploited?

7 A colleague recommends a new management book to you. Do you: a) smile and say you haven't any time for new-fangled ideas; b) thank him and forget about it; c) buy the book?

8 You receive an invitation to attend a management-training course geared at top managers. Do you: a) tell your secretary not to bother you with this sort of rubbish; b) attend the course; c) book a place, then cancel because of pressures of work?

9 You are interviewing a candidate for a management position. Do you ask him or her about: a) work experience; b) golf handicap; c) the management training they've had?

10 You are asked to choose the phrase that best reflects your management style. Is it: a) I get things done; b) I set the course; c) I don't accept excuses?

Scores

1 a) 9; b) 12; c) 2
2 a) 5; b) 9; c) 1
3 a) 2; b) 15; c) 27
4 a) 1; b) 6; c) 5
5 a) 4; b) 9; c) 2
6 a) 4; b) 8; c) 0
7 a) 8; b) 5; c) Thank you very much. To us, you're a Saint!
8 a) 9; b) 1; c) 2 (for trying)
9 a) 2; b) 12; c) 7
10 a) 6; b) 2; c) 11

0 ══ 80

Where are you on the scale? The farther you are to the right, the nearer you are to losing your soul!

et's face it, management is not as easy as some people would have us believe. There is the constant need to find solutions to existing problems, deal with the consequences of old problems, and at the same time think about avoiding new problems. And then, of course, there's the need to create shareholder value, to take steps to improve environmental control, to attract and retain the best employees, to work out the strategy for the coming years, to fight off competition, to look for new opportunities, to maintain motivation, to improve profitability, to implement the latest quality requirements, to work ethically and responsibly, to cut costs and raise income, to build up increased brand awareness and image, and to work on networking. The list, it would seem, is endless.

The manager's lot is not a happy one.

Yet most managers feel they are doing their job as well as can be expected. Of course, there is always room for improvement, but on the whole they are not putting on a bad show. And that show would seem even better if you take into account the unexpected downturn in the market, the latest product that fitted consumer needs like a glove but just didn't take off (but that's marketing for you), and the pressure that ever-decreasing life-cycles and shorter time-to-market puts on the whole company.

What's a manager to do?

Quite simply, he has to fix it. He has to find the fastest, least expensive and most efficient way out of the situation. And then just go for it.

Pride is seldom delicate; it will please itself with very mean advantages.
— Samuel Johnson

It's all down to experience

Is it surprising, then, that the majority of management decisions are based on the experience a manager has built up during his career? Isn't that experience the very thing that makes him so successful at his job? Isn't his proven ability to weather out the storm part of the package that makes him employable?

And indeed, experience can be of inestimable value. Experience in negotiating employment contracts with trade unions can prove an enormous benefit for the company concerned. And the personal network built up over the years can be invaluable when looking for new investors or partners willing to bankroll a new project.

Yet that very same experience can boomerang. The solution proposed can often be one that a manager has used before. The conviction is that if it worked in the past, it will work again today. Circumstances may be different – but the problem is basically the same. So why bother thinking about an alternative approach when there is a tried and proven solution at hand? And anyway, there is simply not enough time to reinvent the wheel every time a new problem arises.

You take pride in your work – and the way you do it!

> *Pride is an admission of weakness;*
> *it secretly fears all competition and dreads all rivals.*
> – Fulton J. Sheen

Good training – wrong curriculum

The problem is that most of today's managers gained their experience working in Industrial Economy companies. And the weapons they use are those learned in an industrial environment. A drop in demand? Then simply downsize. People are little more than hands – and they can be replaced when demand increases again. A new competitor encroaching into your main market? Let's try some price-cutting. The short-term loss can easily be compensated when the competitor throws in the towel and leaves the market to lick his wounds. What about when an overseas competitor suddenly decides to try his hand in an area where there are just a few main players? Well, organise a game of golf and come up with some restrictive measures that will make it extremely difficult to start an operation that has any chance of making a profit.

But such fixes don't work in the Knowledge-based Economy. Downsizing could result in a company losing not only hands, but also brains. And will you be able to get back the best brains if they are sceptical about long-term job prospects? Price-cutting will generally create such a loss that it will be impossible to recoup in a situation where product life-cycles are measured in months rather than years. And ganging up on a competitor? All very well – except that that same competitor could be the ideal partner in your next venture.

New situations in a new economy need new solutions.

We all have to change

How often do managers reach for the weapon of change to solve problems? They talk about the necessity for a new mindset, for new methods of working, for a greater willingness to work differently, for the need for retraining. Yet what they preach they rarely put into practice. Because, they say, they simply don't have the time. And anyway, none of this is a substitute for experience.

Sure – like being an accountant is a great background for doing brain surgery!

Change – and here we are specifically referring to change in attitude and mindset – is something essential as we move resolutely from the Industrial Economy into the Knowledge-based Economy. We must obtain a fresh insight into our business, knowing intimately our company's strengths and weaknesses. We cannot go on as if it is business as usual – because in today's world it is business as *un*usual.

Few managers would say that people can't change because 'we have always done things this way'. Yet managers, although never actually admitting to this, use the very same argument, albeit tacitly. They continue to do things in the way they have always done them. They continue with the managerial status quo.

Did you know that of the Fortune Top 500 companies in 1970, only 4 per cent – yes, just 4 per cent – were still around in the same guise by 1991? You don't move on by staying the same. Either as a company or as a manager.

> *Faced with the choice between changing one's mind and proving that there is no need to do so, almost everyone gets busy on the proof.*
> – John Kenneth Galbraith

Go for success

Of course, there is a conviction that success breeds success. And in some ways this is true. But today, many companies believe that a manager with success in one business can transplant that success into a new company. This is certainly the case in the telecom industry, where job-hopping has become the norm, with Mike Armstrong, Sir Peter Bonfield and Ron Sommer assuming top executive positions in AT&T, BT and Deutsche Telekom respectively without prior experience in the industry. Both Bonfield and Sommer were later ousted as share prices in their companies plummeted.

Although there are, of course, links between the computing and communications industry, one has to wonder whether any of these highly respected managers had a full understanding of the specific challenges and opportunities offered by the telecom industry. Had they been brought in to guide their new companies into the future? Or had they been brought it to mop up the mess of the past?

Most managers would claim the former is true for them; most end up doing the latter.

In *Competing for the Future*, Hamel and Pralahad talk about the typical approach managers adopt in moments of industry or business crisis:

When performance declines, the first assumption is that the company has gotten fat, so investment and headcount are attacked. If this fails to bring about a lasting improvement in performance, as is usually the case, senior managers may conclude that the company has also gotten lazy, and that core processes are rife with needless bureaucracy and 'make-work'. A re-engineering program is adopted with the objective of shaping up sloppy processes. But ... restructuring and re-engineering may ultimately be too little too late ... To get ahead of the industry-change curve ... top management must recognise that the company may be blind as well as fat and lazy. [1]

In other words, managers reach for Industrial Economy tools even when the industry is firmly rooted in the Knowledge-based Economy.

And they do it with pride!

The fellow who thinks he knows it all is
especially annoying to those of us who do.

– Harold Coffin

High profile

Perhaps what it all comes down to is courage. It is certainly easier to adopt a management approach that has been tried and tested for many years. Nobody can fault you for that. And many such approaches are high profile, clearly stamping a mark on the organisation. Managers are not only doing something, they are *seen* to be doing something.

This is reflected in other areas, too. To return again to Hamel and Pralahad:

Many companies rely on big, bold acquisitions and grassroots
'intrapreneurship' for corporate regeneration ... Top management
often sees a major acquisition as the only escape route from a
business that has become hopelessly mature ... Acquisitions are, in
many cases, an easy way out for senior executives too intellectually
lazy to think through the future of the firm's 'core' business and too
unimaginative to discover new ways of deploying existing
capabilities.[2]

But they make great headlines. And they demonstrate to the market – read: stock market – that the company really means business.

This need to be seen to be doing things is reflected very clearly in the rush to get on to the internet. The hype created around the net has convinced many managers that this is the only way forward. Get thee to the internet and find salvation. Yet one wonders how many managers, eager to jump on this latest bandwagon, have really thought through the implications that such a move can have.

Everyone knows about the success of amazon.com. A few entrepreneurs opened a bookshop on the internet and made their fortune. If it happened to them, why shouldn't it happen to us?

The answer is that the website of amazon.com was little more than a portal to a highly efficient and well-managed distribution system. Amazon.com recognised that in the internet world of click-and-go, customers wouldn't be prepared to wait weeks for the delivery of their order. And so their system was geared to providing an immediate response to every order, with full details about expected delivery time. They understood the need for fast response. And they created a system that could guarantee this.

But how many companies on the internet today really offer fast response times? Or understand that a website needs to be backed up by a dedicated system of response? Nothing is more frustrating to a potential customer than to request information and then wait around for some response. The immediacy of the internet requires an immediacy of response. And if that doesn't happen, then there is little chance that a customer will add that particular website to their list of favourites.

Men occasionally stumble on the truth, but most of them pick themselves
up and hurry off as if nothing had happened.

– Sir Winston Churchill

Hype-hopping

In May 2001, the following report was read on *BBC News*: 'A
survey of British and German businesses has revealed that the
majority of them have embarked on e-commerce strategies simply
to make themselves appear modern and forward-looking. But few
of those questioned said that their adoption of e-commerce had
generated big savings or made a big difference to how the company
operated. BT Ignite, which commissioned the survey, says that
unless companies wholeheartedly embrace e-commerce and use it
to change the way they do business, few will get any significant
benefit from it. Adopting an e-commerce strategy, said 71 per cent
of UK companies and 65 per cent of German businesses questioned, made them look more progressive and up-to-date in the
eyes of their customers. Danny Garvey, a spokesman for BT Ignite,
said that many companies seemed to have jumped on the e-commerce bandwagon with little thought about what they were trying
to achieve. In the survey, 25 per cent of respondents in both countries said they had turned to e-commerce for short-term commercial gains, and 50 per cent said there was no business plan to back
up the move to more electronic ways of working.'[3]

In the world of e-commerce, pride certainly did come before
the fall. So why, as this survey shows, do managers rush in where
angels fear to tread? A simple answer would be that some new
trends are so hyped up that they cannot escape the attention of

managers. Managers grab at the possibilities offered by such high-profile trends and jump on the bandwagon so that they won't be left behind. It is, in other words, a way of hedging their management bets.

But there is a much more fundamental reason which has everything to do with priorities. Managers spend their time managing. They try to get more done in the available time. The rise in time-management systems illustrates the overwhelming desire of managers to be 'efficient'. Meetings are kept are short as possible. Proposals have to be reduced to 'no more than one page'. 'In-depth analyses' are out, a 'brief summary of the conclusions' is in. 'Just give me what I need to know,' is the oft-repeated instruction.

A little knowledge can be a dangerous thing. Yet most managers force themselves to reach major decisions based on superficial information. And they will defend this by pointing out that they have excellent staff to do the legwork, leaving them free to do the managing.

Managers today have allowed themselves to be ruled by their schedules. Only a handful – if any – would be willing or prepared to spend more than just a few hours 'getting up to speed' on new management theories or techniques. And so they grasp at the latest hype. Because that is something they can understand quickly and easily. Hypes provide managers with a quick fix. And hey, if it's such a big thing, it can't be bad.

But hypes – just like products – are subject to ever-shorter life-cycles. What is big today is yesterday's news tomorrow. And when hypes fail to produce tangible results, then they are written off.

There is much danger of this happening with the concept of e-commerce. It was a hype, but then became over-hyped, and now managers are turning their backs on it without taking the time to investigate the full implications and possibilities it could provide. If the new hype says that the old hype is dead – then that must be true, too.

Fear of managers

But there is another, far more sinister aspect here. Many CEO high-flyers have – how should we put this? – a forceful personality. Often they put the fear of God into their employees – even those closest to them. Their pride has grown to such proportions that they do not appreciate any reservation about plans they put forward. They manage by force of personality; they do not like anybody to contradict them. Yet in a survey he carried out, psychologist Daniel Goleman concluded that 'higher-ranking executives are less likely to have an accurate assessment of their own performance'. [4]

Fear of the CEO was a contributory factor in the failure of one of Samsung's pet projects. Chairman Lee Kun Hee, a car enthusiast, decided to take Samsung into the overcrowded automobile business. It required an investment of $13 billion, and many executives in the company were anxious about the project and opposed such a large investment. But nobody spoke up. Lee Kun Hee had his way. Just one year into production, however, Samsung Motors folded, and Lee was forced to spend $2 billion of his own money to placate creditors. His response: 'How come nobody spoke up?'[5]

My idea of an agreeable person is a person who agrees with me.

– Benjamin Disraeli

Addressing complexity

Much of this comes down to the reluctance of managers to address complexity. Managers have been used to dealing with either-or situations – to be able to choose to go one way or another. Today, management decisions need to take into account an ever-increasing number of frequently conflicting demands. They are confronted with and-and situations, in which there is no clear answer, no clear indication of the right way ahead. Social responsibility adds a new dimension to the need for cost-effective production. If that is further complicated by the need for environmental control, then the complexity of any decision is vastly increased.

Such complexity cannot be reduced to one-page proposals.

And such complexity faced Shell in the mid-1990s. They had a floating oil warehouse that had become redundant. They decided to sink it. A simple either-or situation. Yet it proved a decision that had far-reaching consequences for the company. A Dutch newspaper reported:

> The Brent Spar paradox shows that companies can no longer make decisions separate from other related developments. The solution to sink the floating oil warehouse into the ocean may have been the best economically, it nevertheless proved socially unacceptable. Environmental concerns expressed by action groups such as Greenpeace and the ensuing public pressure eventually forced Shell to reconsider its decision and look for new solutions to the proposed sinking. As the company's president, Herkströter, said at a seminar in Amsterdam: 'Our technological background, which told us that problems have to be identified, isolated and solved, works well with technological problems, but isn't very useful when confronted with

softer problems. Whereas technical problems may only have one solution, the search for solutions to social and political dilemmas generates many possible answers, which are almost always compromises.'[6]

Compromise? Can managers learn to live with that? It goes against everything they have ever learned. Compromise is a sign of weakness; swift, decisive action is the mark of a true manager.

And it is this very desire to show they can take swift, decisive action that makes managers shy away from complexity. Understanding complexity demands time – and that, for a manager, is the one thing in short supply. It also demands deep insight into the business – not just into products and markets and processes, but also into the core competencies. It means having an intimate knowledge of every aspect of a company's abilities and finding new ways of utilising the knowledge available within the company to find new products, new technologies, new markets.

It means taking action today that will ensure sustainability in the future.

Ach – isn't it easier to concentrate on shareholder value? On meeting quality standards? On tomorrow's financial report? On the next product?

Isn't it better to concentrate on business as usual – rather than on business as unusual?

To be a man's own fool is bad enough; but the vain man is everybody's.

– William Penn

Hands on?

Today's managers often speak proudly of their hands-on style of management. They boast about their grassroots approach to problems. About their decisiveness. Their single-mindedness. And they boast about past successes and how their experience was earned the 'hard way', on the shop floor.

Hands-on management was fine – in the Industrial Economy. But today's Knowledge-based Economy requires something more. It requires, above all, brains-on management. Managers today must be prepared to invest more of their time in knowing, and less in doing. Management – like any other profession – evolves. It is unlikely that Henry Ford could turn around an ailing dot.com company. Times have changed – and everybody is aware of that except, it sometimes seems, managers. For they continue trying to store new wine in old bottles.

Just as engineers are required constantly to update their knowledge if they want to perform in their chosen profession, so managers must spend much more time on re-education, learning and reading what the rest of the world is doing. Certainly it is essential for them to rid their minds of much of the baggage carried over from the Industrial Economy. They must learn *not* to reach automatically for the tools of resizing, re-engineering or restructuring, for by doing so they force their company to take a step backwards rather than one forwards.

Innovator – innovate yourself!

Over the last two decades, we have deconstructed, analysed,

re-engineered, retooled, rethought and innovated in every aspect of business. Every aspect, that is, except the business of management itself. That has been spared change. Management has not been affected by downsizing (there are more managers within companies today than at any other time in the past); and management has most certainly not been affected by an ongoing programme of retraining. Managers today do business in the way they have always done it.

They have innovated in processes, practices and products; they have as yet not dared to innovate in their own work practices.

Yet that innovation, that determination to reinvent the core of management as a profession is needed more today than at any other time in the past. The complexity of the Knowledge-based Economy needs managers who do not allow themselves to remain forever trapped in the industrial era. It needs managers who are prepared to think more than they act, and allow their minds to take quantum leaps into unknown territory.

Management has implemented change, yet it has never submitted itself to change. That would mean substituting humility for pride. And there are very few managers around that are prepared to be humble.

The sad thing is that even the finest business studies courses have failed to identify this. They are still now offering students the same Industrial Economy-based curriculum that has been offered for many, many years. We are seriously concerned that today a degree in business studies could very well do a potential manager more harm than good. It teaches historical business practices; it provides students with the wrong tools for solving problems that have never been encountered in the past.

Pride is at the bottom of all great mistakes.

– John Rushkin

Towards zero-mindedness

Nowadays business, whether we like it or not, demands a totally new approach to management. By holding on to the past, we greatly restrict our own abilities. We allow ourselves to be bound by the harness of history. We allow ourselves to become clones of our predecessors. We lose the desire to maintain our individuality.

The first priority, we believe, of today's managers is to clear their minds of all the unnecessary baggage they carry round with them. They must learn to become zero-minded. They must learn to open their minds to new ideas – but not just superficially, as they have all too often done with hypes. They must be prepared to address the increasing complexity of a business that is no longer based on simple either–or decisions.

And perhaps, most importantly of all, they must understand that people and the thoughts and ideas those people carry in their minds are the true key to continued resilience and sustainability.

Management today is more than at any time in the past about managing people. About creating an environment that encourages a free flow of knowledge. It means breaking down walls between departments and stimulating an exchange of ideas that goes beyond traditional lines of authority.

There is no quick fix for people. Managers who think otherwise are simply deluding themselves. And committing one of the most deadly sins of all.

CASES

The sinner: Management

In the first quarter of 2002, PricewaterhouseCoopers commissioned an independent survey exploring attitudes to business downturn and managing costs. In the survey, published under the title 'Strange Days: Are Businesses Equipped to Catch Opportunity in an Unpredictable World?', 590 businesses with turnovers ranging from $500 million to $5 billion were interviewed in Europe, the Americas, Africa and Australia. [7] Interviews were conducted with senior executives within the business, typically at CFO or equivalent level, across a range of industry sectors. We quote the key results here:

- *Chaos theory has become business reality*: Volatility and unpredictability are facts of life for companies worldwide – illustrated by respondents' lack of agreement over the current economic climate. There's a clear 50/50 split in the number of respondents who said their company was operating in a downturn environment. Our research shows that across industries and geographies there is no clear view of the market or set pattern to attitudes.
- *Short-term cuts to please shareholders, not longer-term strategies to build businesses*: Companies confuse short-term shareholder appeasement with effective cost control. Confronted by economic uncertainty, managers worldwide will all too readily resort to slash–and–burn cost-cutting, instead of approaching cost control strategically for the longer term.
- *Companies are not practising what they preach*: 86 per cent of respondents agree that significant short-term cost reduction pro-

grammes can be strongly detrimental to staff morale and loyalty, and 55 per cent agree that obvious cost cutting is more about impressing analysts and shareholders than improving the business. But knowing this does not stop most companies from making the same short-term cuts they know to be damaging to the longer-term prospects of the business.

- *Too much cost cutting can be fatal, leaving companies under-resourced for the future*: Our survey shows that companies have yet to understand this – quick-fix cost reduction dominates the global agenda, with 60 per cent of companies putting recruitment and investment on hold. Many companies do not appear to have learned the lessons of the early 1990s, and seem intent on making sure history repeats itself – in other words, companies seem to be applying lessons learned during very different economic times.

- *Weeding out costs will not stop them from growing back*: 57 per cent of respondents agree that the costs they are currently cutting will be back in their organisations within two to three years – short-term solutions rarely attack the root of the problem.

The saint: ST Microelectronics

The semiconductor industry has not been going through an easy period. The year 2001 saw a drastic reduction in sales – down 32 per cent – setting off massive cost-cutting operations, staff lay-offs and curtailment of investment plans throughout the industry. Except, it seems, at ST Microelectronics. There, management has done everything possible to avoid using the blunt tools of industrial-age thinking.

ST Microelectronics was formed in 1987 from state-owned entities in France and Italy. It has been publicly trading since 1994, with 45 per cent of its stock equally divided between the governments of France and Italy. It is now a multinational enterprise, employing some 40,000 people in twenty-seven countries, nearly half of whom work in France and Italy. The Agrate site, near Milan – which employs around 12 per cent of the total workforce – operates as a manufacturing plant and is also the centre for all R&D activities.

ST Microelectronics has gained a reputation as a good employer. It may not pay the highest wages in the industry, but it manages to retain its talent thanks to an environment that they describe as challenging, friendly and stimulating.

All this does not mean it has not been affected by the downturn in the market. But it has influenced the way the company reacted. Instead of implementing wide-scale lay-offs that typified the management approach of many other companies in the industry, ST Microelectronics developed a range of measures aimed at avoiding such a step. These included incentive severance packages and natural staff reduction – but these also included pay cuts for the executives. Management was prepared to do its share in helping the company – and its employees. Thanks to the positive feeling that pervades the company – and the awareness among employees that management is prepared to share in their pain – there is a determination to succeed. In 1995, ST was ranked number fourteen in the list of worldwide chip-makers; by 2000, it had moved up to the sixth position.

Postlude

Regaining Credibility

Is there any hope of gaining absolution?

We started this book by stating that managers and management are losing their credibility. We believe the Seven Deadly Sins we have discussed show to what extent this is true. There is a growing greed in boardrooms. And, more distressingly, an increasing dehumanisation. Managers have allowed themselves to fall into the trap of approaching every problem coolly. Dispassionately.

Managers have lost their passion for people.

Many organisations today are still firmly rooted in the industrial past. They have developed against a background of mature markets, complex industrial processes and five-year business plans. They are hierarchical, cumbersome, inflexible and lethargic. They are the dinosaurs of business. The recent internet failures made many old companies believe the dinosaurs had won — but have they? In the Knowledge-based Economy, business dinosaurs may make a noise, but they will find it difficult to make a profit. The speed of innovation, the shortening of product cycles, the complexity of offerings required by an increasingly demanding consumer – all these require organisations that are 'all brains and no body'. Non-brain body weight is kept to an absolute minimum; all other processes are outsourced or eliminated entirely. It's the 'all brain processes' that add value to a company. They are the intangible assets that make up a company's weightless wealth.

Ask the question

So how do we break out of this situation? Well, the first step is simply to ask the question 'What's on the other side' – to apply our natural curiosity to our business.

You see, many of the limits in our company are not built with bricks. They are not tangible structures. You cannot point to them. You cannot take a sledgehammer to them. Because most of the limits are simply in our minds. We create them. Maintain them. Give them an indestructibility they do not really have.

So if they exist only in our minds, then that is the place we have to clear first.

'Oh yes,' we hear you say. 'It's all right for you to talk – you don't have to face the fights, the obstructions, the difficulties that I have to face every day.'

That's where you're wrong. We fight the same fights as you. Every single day. Dealing with a lack of co-operation. A lack of sharing. Dealing with inflexibility, lack of decisiveness, an inability to get things done now, rather than in six weeks' time. All the things that any manager, anywhere, has to deal with.

But we also know that these things won't go away unless you take the first step towards obtaining the biggest weapon you can have: zero-mindedness

Nelson Mandela is reported to have said that although his political opponents could imprison his body, they could never imprison his mind. Yet many of us in business allow our minds to be imprisoned by old-time, industrial age thinking. We tell ourselves that things were always done like this. That the organisation was designed to help the business. That divisions are natural. That it makes economic sense for each division, unit, whatever you call it, to be regarded as an individual profit-centre.

Deep down, however, we know that we are only fooling ourselves. We know that our rigid organisational structure is stifling our business. Preventing close co-operation between people who may be doing the same work, but are located in different departments – even, as globalisation increases, in different continents. Organisational and geographical boundaries have conspired to keep us trapped.

We've allowed ourselves to become victims of the tyranny of the pigeon-hole.

What we mean by becoming zero-minded is simply that we need to let go of all these restricting preconceptions. To empty our minds of the barriers that exist there. To learn to ask, 'What's on the other side?'

Regain the passion

The job of manager used to be an honourable profession. Managers made a difference. To business. To the community. To people.

Today, it seems, they only care about making a difference to the balance sheet. And to the value of their own stock options.

In his article 'Managing quietly', Henry Mintzberg, Professor of Management Studies at McGill University in Montreal, writes:

> *Quiet managers don't empower their people – empowerment is taken for granted. They inspire them. They create the conditions that foster openness and release energy ... Quiet managers strengthen the cultural bonds between people by not treating them as detachable 'human resources' (probably the most offensive terms ever coined in management, at least until 'human capital' came along), but as respected members of a cohesive social system. When people are trusted, they do not have to be empowered.*[1]

Have we gone too far down the road of dehumanisation ever to regain our passion for people? The simple truth is that if management is to regain its credibility, passion is the one thing that is required. Forget processes. Forget shareholders. Forget greed.

And learn to nurture people.

For if we continue taking people out of the business equation, then we will continue sinning. And then we will have to learn to live with the consequences.

Notes

The First Deadly Sin: Lust in the Boardroom

1 http://www.kennedyinfo.com/ir/svm/svm.html
2 S. Davis and C. Meyer, *Blur*, Capstone Publishing Ltd, 1998
3 Daniel Andriessen and René Tissen, *Weightless Wealth*, Pearson Education Ltd, 2000
4 http://www.kennedyinfo.com/ir/svm/svm.html
5 http://www.isb.is/english/vsm_isl/owa/disp.birta-pk=115.htm
6 Cadbury Schweppes Annual Report, 2001
7 http://www.archcoal.com/xpedio/groups/public/documents/aci_internet/ci_index.html
8 http://www.hillenbrand.com/about_hb.html
9 http://www.secure.paconsulting.com/pac/msv/msvsur.html
10 http://www.investor.philips.com/reporting/AR98/pres.htm
11 http://www.investor.philips.com/reporting/AR99/pres.htm
12 http://www.investor.philips.com/reporting/AR98/pres.htm
13 http://www.investor.philips.com/reporting/AR99/pres.htm

14 Ram Charan and Jerry Useem, 'Why companies fail', *Fortune*, 27 May, 2002

15 *ibid*.

16 'A gift for much more than cosmetic change', *Financial Times*, 26 June 2001

17 *ibid*.

18 Erin Davis, 'Shareholders aren't everything', *Fortune*, February 1997

The Second Deadly Sin: Wrath on the High Street

1 Louis Lavelle, 'The case of the corporate spy', *Business Week*, 26 November 2001

2 'From the nexus of Lexus', *Business Week*, 24 September 2001

3 Lavelle, 'The case of the corporate spy'

4 *ibid*.

5 'P&G to seek new resolution of spy dispute', *Financial Times*, 3 September 2001

6 'Fear of the unknown', *Economist*, 2 December 1999

7 'Core business: Bedrijven weten maar half waar ze echt goed in zijn' (Companies only know half of what they are good at), *Management Team*, 9 September 2001

8 'Intel: Can CEO Craig Barrett reverse the slide?', *Business Week*, 15 October 2001

9 *ibid*.

10 'Unilever explores new niche in Brazil', *Adage.com*, 3 January 2001

11 'Smart globalization', *Business Week*, 27 August 2001

12 Metro sets stage for global newspaper war', *Adage.com*, 30 April 2001

13 R. Lewin and B. Regine, *The Soul at Work*, Orion Business Books, 1999

14 J. F. Moore, 'The new corporate form', in *Blueprint to the Digital Economy*, D. Tapscott, A. Lowy and D. Ticoll, New York, McGraw-Hill, 1998

15 Lewin and Regine, *The Soul at Work*

16 Compiled from various articles published on www.bbc.co.uk

The Third Deadly Sin: Sloth in Executive Decisions

1 Alvin Toffler, *Future Shock* (1970), Bantam Books, 1991

2 Gary Hamel and C. K. Pralahad, *Competing for the Future*, Harvard Business School Press, 1994

3 Stastisitcs compiled from B. R. Mitchell, *International Historical Statistics Europe 1750–1988*, New York, 1992, pp. 913–19; *International Historical Statistics The Americas 1750–1988*, New York, 1993, pp. 775–81; and *International Historical Statistics Africa, Asia & Oceania 1950–1988*, New York, 1995, pp. 1022–32

4 *BBC News*, 23 July 1999

5 *BBC News*, 25 July 2001

6 Ram Charan and Jerry Useem, 'Why companies fail,' *Fortune* 27 May 2002

7 *BBC News*, 25 May 1999

8 *BBC News*, 24 May 1999

9 http://news.bbc.co.uk/1/hi/business/1269274.stm

10 Keynote speech given at the ISS Conference in 1998

11 Dan Roberts, 'The world caught third-generation fever' *Financial Times*, 5 September 2001

12 http://www.bertelsmann.com
13 *ibid*.

The Fourth Deadly Sin: Covetousness of the Corporate Joneses

1 http://leadership.wharton.upenn.edu/welcome/index.shtml
2 'Guru downsizing heeft zich vergist' (Downsizing guru admits mistake), *De Standaard*, 14 May 1996
3 *ibid*.
4 Peter Scott-Morgan, *Unwritten Rules of the Game*, quoted in 'Change the rules,' M. May, *Information Strategy*, April 1997
5 Information adapted from 'Gebrandmerkt' (Branded), *Fem de Week*, week 44, 2001
6 'Groenink regrets letter to personnel', *NRC Handelsblad*, 20 December 2001
7 'JP Morgan axes jobs as it seeks 20% cut in costs', *Financial Times*, 26 August 2001
8 'Merrill Lynch to offer staff year's pay to resign', *Financial Times*, 19 October 2001
9 Milton Moskowitz and Robert Levering, '10 great companies in Europe: Skandia', *Fortune*, 4 February 2002
10 Peter Martin, 'Buying an experience', *Financial Times*, 14 September 1999
11 Milton Moskowitz and Robert Levering, '10 great companies in Europe: Nokia', *Fortune*, 4 February 2002

The Fifth Deadly Sin: Gluttony for Growth

1 'Fear of the unknown', *Economist*, 2 December 1999
2 'Cisco European chief offers a steadying hand', *Financial Times*, 18 November 2001
3 Ram Charan and Jerry Useem, 'Why companies fail', *Fortune*, 27 May 2002
4 'Innovation still valued at technology companies', *Industry Week*, 23 August 2001
5 'Will the corporation survive?' *Economist,* 1 November 2000
6 Gary Hamel and C. K. Pralahad, *Competing for the Future*, Harvard Business School Press, 1994
7 'Will the corporation survive?'
8 'Tweedehuisjesmelkers' (Making money out of second houses), *HP de Tijd*, 9 November 2001
9 'Will the corporation survive?'
10 'Genfit signs agreement with BMPF and Fournier', *La Tribune*, France; 23 November 2001
11 'Will the corporation survive?'
12 'Alcatel launches a worldwide Research Partnership Program', Alcatel press release, 1 October 2001
13 *ibid.*
14 http://news.bbc.co.uk/hi/english/business

The Sixth Deadly Sin: Envy in the Workplace

1 'Co\$t Vs Quality', *Industry Week*, 9 January 2001
2 *ibid.*
3 Gary Hamel and C. K. Pralahad, *Competing for the Future*,

Harvard Business School Press, 1994

4 Richard E. S. Boulton, Barry D. Libert and Steve M. Samek, *Cracking the Value Code*, Harper Business, 2000

5 'Sea of IP – an interview with Theo Classen', produced for Philips Semiconductors by Jonathan Ellis BV, 2000

The Seventh Deadly Sin: Pride at the Top

1 Gary Hamel and C.K. Pralahad, *Competing for the Future*, Harvard Business School Press, 1994

2 *ibid*.

3 *BBC News*, 3 May 2001

4 Quoted in: 'Why companies fail', Ram Charan and Jerry Useem, *Fortune*, 27 May 2002

5 *ibid*.

6 'Herkströter: Shell ondanks arrogantie bolwerk integriteit' (Herkströter: Shell, despite arrogance, stronghold of integrity), Holland, *Het Financiele Dagblad*, 12 October 1996

7 'Strange days: Are businesses equipped to catch opportunity in an unpredictable world?', survey PricewaterhouseCoopers, 2002

Postlude: Regaining Credibility

1 Henry Mintzberg, 'Managing quietly', *Leader to Leader*, No. 12, Spring 1999

Index